Kitchen Garden Cook Book

By the same author

FARMHOUSE KITCHEN
WINE LOVERS COOKBOOK
COOKING TO MAKE KIDS SLIM

Kitchen Garden Cook Book

Honey · Herbs · Flowers and Fruit · Vegetables

Audrey Ellis

With drawings by Kate Simunek

STANLEY PAUL/LONDON

Stanley Paul & Co Ltd
3 Fitzroy Square, London W1

An imprint of the Hutchinson Publishing Group

London Melbourne Sydney Auckland
Wellington Johannesburg and agencies
throughout the world

First published 1972
Second impression June 1977
© Audrey Ellis 1972
Drawings © Stanley Paul 1972

Printed in Great Britain by litho at The Anchor Press Ltd
and bound by Wm Brendon & Son Ltd
both of Tiptree, Essex

ISBN 0 09 117701 3

Contents

Introduction

King Alfred was not renowned as a cook, but he was an authority on the use of herbs. Perhaps he sat crouched over the charcoal burner's hearth, absorbed more in the fascinating study of his great *Leech Book* than in his country's problems, when he allowed the famous cakes to burn. This formidable tome was said to have listed the healing and culinary uses of some five hundred herbs, all of which grew in Britain before the Normans came.

In the cleared patch outside his cottage, the charcoal burner probably cultivated some of these herbs, especially the strongly flavoured ones such as garlic, onions and leek, 'well-liked' by Chaucer's Sompnour in the *Canterbury Tales*. There would have been coriander, parsley and fennel; violets and clumps of primroses, transplanted from the woods to add a piquant touch to salads, and to make the traditional Easter treat of pottage, flower heads stewed in milk and honey. No wall or fence enclosed such a garden. Wild rose briars made a natural hedge, providing fragrant petals for colouring and flavouring food, and a safe anchorage for household linen on the rare occasions when it was washed. Straw skeps of bees yielded all the sweetness a cottager could command for cooking, since sugar was as yet unknown in this country.

Medicinal herbs were given little space, for sickly peasants visited the herbarium of the nearest monastery, the only real garden of that day, to benefit from the Sacristan's blessing as well as his herbal remedies. More often still they risked damnation by swallowing potions brewed by the local wise woman, also from herbs, but made more effective by whispering a spell or adding some nauseous ingredient to the concoction.

This small patch of ground, hedged with briar and apple or cherry trees, furnished with wild fruit bushes and vegetables we would now call weeds, was the forerunner of the kitchen garden.

As social conditions in Britain changed, the landless serf became an independent labourer who grew food for his family's needs in the enclosed garden of his rented cottage, and then in time an artisan forced to abandon the country for a town life. So deeply ingrained was the urge to gather food of his own growing that a mill-hand, for instance, would willingly journey outside the town to an allotment for which he paid a guinea a year, when a guinea represented more than a man's weekly wage.

With time, the urge has faded, but not disappeared. Today's Britons who work with their hands or wear white collars still enjoy a deep satisfaction in gardening, and seeing their families eat produce untouched by chemical aids not of their choosing.

In King Alfred's day, cottage fare was monotonous. Dark bread, cheese, salt porridge or milk puddings made of barley and sweetened with honey. Green salads such as watercress straight from the brook, and green stews of any vegetables and herbs that could be dug up by the roots and persuaded to grow near the doorstep.

The idea of growing plants for beauty rather than for use introduced by the Romans had vanished with them, along with their sophisticated standard of living. But gradually, flowering plants began to find a place, at first mainly for their value in flavouring. Some grew wild, or had been introduced at an earlier date in history, as cherries were by the Romans; or arrived with the Norman invaders, like the clove-scented pink, whose flowers were used to impart their spicy fragrance to drinks. During Chaucer's lifetime the pink was grown in every ale-house garden. Flowers also had another important function, that of releasing their sweet scents when dried or distilled to make flower oils and essences used in the kitchen, for medicinal purposes, and for beauty. Perfumed waters were given as presents on Saints' days and birthdays, much as they are today. Cottage interiors were damp, dark, crowded with cooking odours and other smells far from inviting. Aromatic herbs were grown for use, like rushes, to strew over the floors. Chief among them were southernwood and wormwood which kept away fleas; hyssop, and rue with its resinous scent flavoured with orange; sage and lavender, the dried stems of which were burnt like incense.

As new plants came to be introduced, they were set wherever space could be found for them. Thus the cottage garden became a place of delightful disorder. Green cabbages neighboured with cabbage roses, daffodils with onions, and close by grew marigolds, whose bright petals were in demand for onion stews and salads.

Spices were never a success. Though attempts to grow them were made by the Romans and later by Crusaders returning from the East, our temperate climate and lack of sun gave them a poor welcome. Spices remained an expensive imported commodity, and few ever became natives of our own kitchen gardens.

In the sixteenth century, kitchen gardens began to take on a more orderly appearance, with the introduction of such arrangements as the 'knotted' bed, by which dwarf box, thrift or marjoram hedges were used (often in the most intricate designs) to contain plants of a compact habit. Sometimes, gardens were more simply divided by low clipped borders of useful rosemary or lavender. During the next two hundred years, the layout of the typical small kitchen garden became less severe than the Tudor ideal, but never reverted to the artless confusion of an earlier age. Usually a bold show of flowers edged a neat path from front gate to door, and the rest of the space was devoted to herbs, vegetables, fruit trees and bushes in serried rows—paths were planned for easy cultivation rather than to produce a harmonious vista. So it has remained, with a cold frame, or greenhouse for tomatoes to complete the picture.

Every country cook had, as the year progressed, all these good things at her disposal. In summer, potatoes, peas, beans, lettuces, cucumbers, beetroot, radishes, onions, carrots, rhubarb, gooseberries, red and black currants, strawberries, raspberries, apples, pears, plums, damsons, cherries, even peaches, nectarines and figs. The herb garden contained parsley, chives, mint, marjoram, thyme, rosemary and lavender at the very least. Many fruits and herbs were preserved or dried for winter use, when on came turnips, parsnips, leeks, cauliflowers, celery, white and red cabbage, spinach and kale. All these I grow in my own garden.

The meals an eighteenth-century housewife could produce were not as exotic, perhaps, as those we enjoy nowadays but they were satisfying, well seasoned and varied. Delicate custards, rich with cream and scented with marigold petals or rose geranium leaves followed a roast or game pie redolent of herbs which often grew under the dining-room window. Soups were the quintessence of garden vegetables, and sauces subtly flavoured. Country cooking was an art in which much pride was taken, from the lodge keeper's kitchen to the great hall of the manor house. Some of the recipes given in this book date from this period, or even earlier.

I have a cherished childhood memory of my favourite kitchen garden. Oddly enough, not that which belonged to my favourite uncle, the country parson I have referred to in my introduction to *Farmhouse Kitchen*, but that which belonged to his gardener,

9

Saul. Saul was a taciturn bachelor; devoted equally to the Vicarage hothouse and the best asparagus beds, he was certain, in all Sussex. I was terrified of him at first for he reminded me strongly of Mr. McGregor, who held Peter Rabbit at bay in the potting shed. But we became friends, and he kindly made me a little mint garden all my own, including spearmint, apple mint, and eau-de-cologne, and showed me how to recognise each leaf by its scent, shape and texture. As a great treat, I was taken to tea at his cottage one Sunday afternoon.

We had a sponge cake, baked in a tin lined with rose geranium leaves, from the pot on the window sill, to give it a perfumed flavour. Scones with a comb of honey from his own bees, tasting as the Sussex turf smells, of thyme; and a rhubarb tansy with cream. Saul grew his rhubarb under old buckets, forcing it to a pale pink splendour. The cream, I suspect, came from the Vicarage cow.

His garden was square, with the cottage close to the front at one corner; built of stone, the walls inlaid in patterns like knitting with round pebbles from Pevensey beach. The short front path was edged with cockle shells, and a border of frilly parsley set off the beds of standard roses, sweet williams and clove pinks. Behind the thick, chunky wall grew all the flowers I was taught to embroider on tray cloths: hollyhocks, larkspur and lupins. Climbing roses, red one side and pink the other, met over the porch—so old, their main stems were thick as my wrist and black with age. Herbs sat snug in the border under the windows and all round the house, except for bay, lavender and rosemary, which formed a thick hedge. Beyond lay the fruit bushes and raspberry canes. Then came the vegetables, in exquisitely neat and well-hoed rows, the beehives, and the cold frame for raising seedlings.

Saul grew enough produce of the highest quality to feed a family, out of pride of ownership, giving most of it away. He used no fertiliser but farmyard manure and his own compost heap. In these days when scientific cultivation brings such dubious benefits it is good to remember him.

If you have a garden, you also can have the satisfaction of growing and knowing what you eat; but if you have to shop for the ingredients in supermarkets or choose to do so in a health food store, I hope you will still enjoy my collection of country recipes.

AUDREY ELLIS

A change is being made in marking oven temperatures. This chart gives the Celsius (formerly Centigrade) equivalents to Fahrenheit temperatures suggested by the Electricity Council.

Description	Gas Mark	°Fahrenheit	°Celsius
Very Cool	Low	200	100
Very Cool	$\frac{1}{4}$	225	110
Cool	$\frac{1}{2}$	250	130
Very Slow	1	275	140
Very Slow	2	300	150
Slow	3	325	170
Moderate	4	350	180
Moderately Hot	5	375	190
Moderately Hot	6	400	200
Hot	7	425	220
Very Hot	8	450	230
Extremely Hot	9	475	240

Note: This chart is only a guide and all cookers vary, so it is important to follow the manufacturer's instructions for your particular cooker, especially if it is of a new type.

Metrication

With the advent of metrication in the near future it is a good idea to understand the principles involved.

At the time of writing it is generally agreed that we should use 25 grammes to the ounce as the nearest easily workable figure instead of the exact conversion of 28·35 grammes for solid measures; and 500 millilitres to the pint, the exact conversion being 568 millilitres. As both these measures are slightly less than the exact conversion it ensures that solid and liquid measures are kept in proportion. This has been proved by experiments to be a satisfactory method, e.g. the basic ingredients for white sauce:

Imperial	Metric
1 OZ. BUTTER	25 GM. BUTTER
1 OZ. FLOUR	25 GM. FLOUR
$\frac{1}{2}$ PINT MILK	250 ML. MILK

Approximate liquid measures: Thin liquids such as water, vinegar, milk, may be measured by the following equivalents:

1 teaspoon	$\frac{1}{6}$ fl. oz.	5 ml.
1 tablespoon	$\frac{1}{2}$ fl. oz.	15 ml.
2 tablespoons	1 fl. oz.	25 ml.
4 tablespoons	$2\frac{1}{2}$ fl. oz.	65 ml.
8 tablespoons	5 fl. oz. ($\frac{1}{4}$ pint)	125 ml.
16 tablespoons	$\frac{1}{2}$ pint	250 ml.
32 tablespoons	1 pint	500 ml.

American Measures: The most important difference to note is that the Imperial pint measures 20 fluid ounces, as compared with the American pint which measures 16 fluid ounces. The American standard measuring cup contains 8 fluid ounces.

General Measures: Unless otherwise stated, throughout this book all spoon measures are level, all recipes serve four.

3 teaspoons—1 tablespoon   1 British Imperial pint—20 fl. oz.
8 tablespoons—$\frac{1}{4}$ pint   1 British Imperial cup—10 fl. oz.
                                                  ($\frac{1}{2}$ pint)

Recipe Guide: In some of the older recipes, ingredients have been altered to modernise and simplify the method.

Some Vegetable Yields

The following figures can only be approximate, as an average yield varies according to the local soil, the position of the garden and seasonal variations.

Broad Beans: $\frac{1}{2}$ pint of seeds averages 30 lb. beans.
Onions: 2 rows each 30 feet gives an average 140 bulbs.
Parsnips: 2 rows each 30 feet gives an average 60 lb. roots.
Peas: 1 pint packet can yield 40 lb. peas.
Beetroot: 1 row, 30 feet, averages 35 lb. roots.
Potatoes: 56 lb. seed yields on average 360 lb. potatoes.
French Beans: $\frac{1}{2}$ pint averages 28 lb. yield of beans.
Runner Beans: 1 row, 30 feet, can yield about 1 cwt. beans.
Brussels Sprouts: About 3 lb. sprouts from each plant.

Planning a kitchen garden

If you have a large garden you should have no difficulty including in your flower borders those which have a culinary use, such as peonies, roses, marigolds and nasturtiums. There will be ample space for growing herbs, and room for a useful-sized, sunny kitchen garden without encroaching on the pleasure garden.

However, with careful planning and management, even a small garden can have a vegetable plot without spoiling its appearance; give a yield of fresh vegetables all the year round and make the time spent on it truly worthwhile. My experience has shown that a family of four can grow much of their fruit and vegetable requirements in an area of 25 feet by 30 feet.

In locating the vegetable and fruit gardens, bear in mind that they should have full sun. Plan vegetable rows to run north to south (to ensure even distribution of sunshine on either side). Keep fruit and vegetables separate. Where there is a choice of positions the best one is that which is high and well-drained, and not overshadowed by buildings or trees. The ideal site is of rectangular shape with walls as boundaries·on north and east sides and a gentle slope towards the west and south. The paths can then be laid so that the sun has the fullest effect upon the crops.

An obvious way of utilising an ideal site would be to have fruit trees growing near the walls, perhaps with espalier pears and peaches trained on the end wall, facing south. In front of these could be a raised vegetable border and then a path. The rest of the plot might consist of two beds, separated by a path, one for soft fruits, another for vegetables and rhubarb, etc. Each bed could have a border of herbs along the dividing path for easy picking. The vegetable and fruit plot might be separated from the pleasure garden by a trellis for climbing roses, clematis and honeysuckle; a border in front with flowers and herbs, and a narrow path behind. But the ideal is seldom practicable for there are other needs to be considered. Compost heap, frames, the inevitable rubbish corner, as well as a tool shed, must be put somewhere, although if possible the sunny spots ought to be utilised to the full.

The main difficulty in a small garden is to get a good 'vista' or impression of distance, but it is not always necessary to put the kitchen garden at the end of a plot, and in broad gardens or plots of irregular shape the vegetables can often go at the side. Avoidance of straight lines is also a help in creating the idea of space. In fact the useful part of the garden can be part of the landscape design.

The majority of inter-war and post-war semi-detached houses have a back garden in the region of 20–30 feet by 60–75 feet; of course, there are many variations, for example, groups of tunnel backs with smaller gardens and detached houses with much larger ones. However, many new council estates and private developments are built to the regulation standard giving only 35 feet back garden length to each house. So it seems realistic to plan a model garden to dimensions of approximately 25 by 65 feet.

The plans on the opposite page and on page 17 are designed by Elizabeth Driver, a planner/landscape architect working as Senior Research Associate with Professor Harry Thorpe, Head of the Department of Geography, University of Birmingham, and Chairman of the Departmental Committee of Inquiry into Allotments. I am indebted to Professor Thorpe for his help and advice on allotment and garden matters generally.

Jointly, Professor Thorpe and Mrs. Driver have been responsible for the design of new style leisure garden sites all over the country, and have advised many local authorities on the rationalisation of their allotment systems.

The leisure garden is a useful allotment combined with a pleasure garden, on a site landscaped to include such facilities as a community centre, and a children's play area, making it a pleasant place for a family outing and giving an opportunity to flat dwellers and others with inadequate gardens to grow their own produce.

The first need, whatever the size of your kitchen plot, is to carry out some simple system of rotation of crops. To grow the same crop year after year in the same piece of ground invites diseases and pests, and generally impoverishes the soil. Big growers adopt elaborate systems of rotation, but the amateur with a small garden can content himself with a simple change-over system shown in the following plan.

Divide your vegetable garden into three sections: A, B and C. Decide on a three year rota and change the crops around each season as shown in the chart given on page 16:

NUMERICAL KEY

1 Shrubs with seasonal interest
2 Lawn
3 Patio/paving slabs of various sizes
4 Red cedar summerhouse
5 Hedged plot boundary
6 Fine gravel path
7 Greenhouse
8 Propagating frames
9 Herb garden hedged with bay
10 Vegetable and salad crops
11 Bush fruits – apple or plum or pear
12 Outdoor storage of equipment
13 Composting area
14 Soft fruits – red or black currants or gooseberries
15 Soft fruits raspberries or strawberries
16 Trellis with climbing roses
17 Shrubs forming visual screen
18 Informal evergreen hedge as visual screen and windbreak
19 Light-foliaged ornamental tree
20 Climbers along dividing fence
21 Mixed herbaceous plants and annuals for culinary use

This plot is planned for a leisure gardener who wishes to cultivate both crops and ornamental plants.

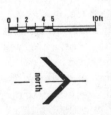

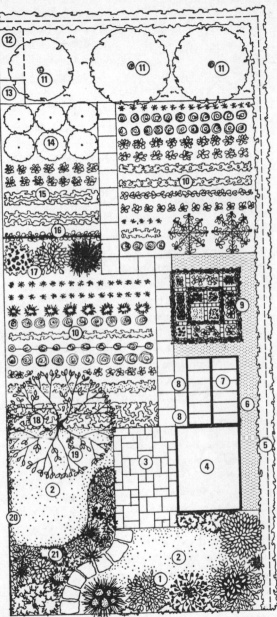

E B Driver M R T P I, Dip LA.

Design for a small leisure garden plot

15

Plot	First Year	Second Year	Third Year
A	Root Crops (No Manure)	Potatoes or beans and peas (Manure or Compost)	Cabbages, sprouts, cauliflowers, etc. (Manure in Autumn)
B	Cabbages, sprouts, cauliflowers, etc. (Manure in Autumn)	Root Crops (No Manure)	Potatoes or beans and peas (Manure or Compost)
C	Potatoes or beans and peas (Manure or Compost)	Cabbages, sprouts, cauliflowers, etc. (Manure in Autumn)	Root Crops (No Manure)

Next, as far as space allows, plan for a succession of vegetables all the year round. Avoid having a glut of one sort of vegetable one month and nothing at all the next. For the non-keeping vegetables, adopt a system of 'successional sowing' according to your space. Sow only a small pinch of lettuce and radish seed at a time, but repeat every two or three weeks from March to September. This also applies to summer spinach, and sow only one or two rows of peas at a time, and follow with others of later varieties. There are cabbage varieties for all seasons of the year.

Where space is very limited you must be ruthlessly selective, cutting out for preference those vegetables that are least economical to grow oneself. The first to omit (on these grounds) is potatoes, which take up a lot of room and are reasonably cheap in the shops. You might, however, like to grow a couple of rows of 'earlies' as a special treat, for, as with other vegetables, they have more flavour when eaten soon after digging. Marrows, courgettes and similar trailing vegetables, take up little space in a bed, but need space to travel so that they can be profitably planted on or near the compost heap. Another tip for limited spaces is to concentrate first on the vegetables of winter when they are at their most expensive in the shops. This means chiefly cabbages, sprouts, broccoli and winter turnips, leeks, parsnips, winter spinach, celery, together with the 'keeper' vegetables; mainly carrots, onions and potatoes if you decide to grow them.

Your choice of what to grow might be determined by the yield you could expect. Runner beans, for instance, can give an im-

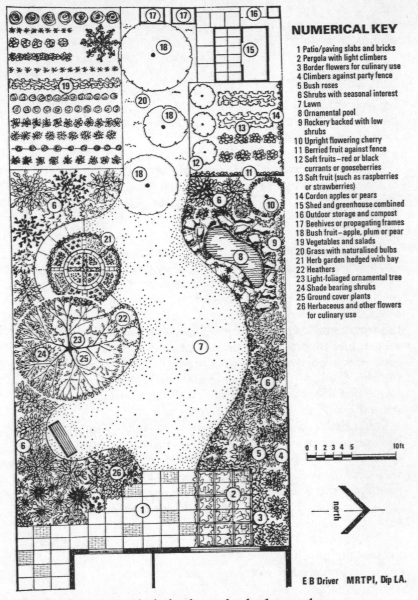

NUMERICAL KEY

1 Patio/paving slabs and bricks
2 Pergola with light climbers
3 Border flowers for culinary use
4 Climbers against party fence
5 Bush roses
6 Shrubs with seasonal interest
7 Lawn
8 Ornamental pool
9 Rockery backed with low shrubs
10 Upright flowering cherry
11 Berried fruit against fence
12 Soft fruits – red or black currants or gooseberries
13 Soft fruit (such as raspberries or strawberries)
14 Cordon apples or pears
15 Shed and greenhouse combined
16 Outdoor storage and compost
17 Beehives or propagating frames
18 Bush fruit – apple, plum or pear
19 Vegetables and salads
20 Grass with naturalised bulbs
21 Herb garden hedged with bay
22 Heathers
23 Light-foliaged ornamental tree
24 Shade bearing shrubs
25 Ground cover plants
26 Herbaceous and other flowers for culinary use

0 1 2 3 4 5   10 ft

north

E B Driver   MRTPI, Dip LA.

Design for an attractively landscaped suburban garden

mensely heavy crop in the region of 10 lb. per yard run. Broad beans do not give a big yield for the land used—a 30 foot row will yield only 15 lb. of Windsors or 11–12 lb. of longpod type, and you need at least 2½ lb. unshelled beans to make a meal for four people. One 30 foot row of perpetual spinach is enough to keep an average family supplied. You may expect an average yield of broccoli of about 6 oz. from each plant at each picking, and before the plant is finished you can have four pickings, but an early variety (late summer) yields more heavily than this. On an average you can expect about 1½ lb. kale from each plant.

However, experienced gardeners can often increase the yield by choosing the variety of seed particularly suitable for their soil, using the organic food required, patient work with the hoe and, for example, plucking off the growing tops of plants such as beans at the right time.

These suggestions are based purely on economic grounds, but it is equally important that you should enjoy your garden by growing the things that you most like. Also, it is worthwhile trying some of the more unusual vegetables not easily found in the shops, such as celeriac, root vegetables that can be left in the ground during the winter and dug as required. Then there are others like kohl-rabi, Jerusalem artichokes, chicory or Belgian endive, and sweet-corn which looks so exotic growing in an English garden. Also, instead of ordinary peas you might like to try sugar peas or *mange tout*, which are most economical as well as a gourmet's delight, for you eat the tender pods with the peas.

Other dodges for making full use of ground are inter-cropping and catch-cropping. Inter-cropping means sowing a quick-maturing vegetable (spinach, radishes, lettuces) between rows of slow-growing ones (celery, leeks, winter cabbage, etc.) before they have approached maturity. Catch-cropping means sowing a quick crop in a plot of ground from which one main crop has been harvested and before another main crop is sown.

Seed catalogues can be a great help in working out times for sowing and harvesting, and a bibliography of useful books to help beginners in vegetable growing is given on page 158.

HONEY

The history of honey is an absorbing subject. Again and again it is mentioned in the Bible and other far older records. Among a series of prehistoric rock paintings found near Valencia, one showed how honey was taken from a wild bees' nest. Painted about 15,000 years ago it shows two people scaling a cliff on a woven ladder to reach the nest; one is holding a primitive 'smoker' to keep the bees away while he removes the honeycombs, and the other is behind him ready to receive the sweet plunder. The bees are drawn as if larger than the men to emphasise the danger they are in.

Honey through the ages

In the early civilisations honey was venerated as a unique food, medicine and mystical symbol of long life and happiness. Eastern races believed in its aphrodisiac powers; many old recipes for love potions show that basically they were made from honey, probably relying on its qualities as a quick source of energy.

The Bible gives many references to honey both as a food and a source of sweetness. Among the Bedouin tribes, today, there are nomadic beekeepers, that is beekeepers who move their bees from place to place in search of honey crops; a system that has probably survived from the days of the wandering tribes of Israel.

The ancient Greeks thought honey sacred, and believed that it held the secret not only of long life but also of perpetual youth. All the Greek Gods feasted on nectar and ambrosia; and Eros, the God of Love, dipped his arrows in honey. Greek athletes were given honey as part of their diet, and water sweetened with it instead of wine as a drink.

The Romans were great beekeepers and appreciators of honey. It figured in most of their religious festivals and feasts. Lucullus savoured a dish of larks' tongues in honey! A pagan belief shared by Romans, Egyptians and Greeks alike attributed the power to increase fertility, as well as other magical properties, to honey.

When Pliny visited Britain he wrote, 'These islanders consume great quantities of honey brew,' meaning mead. Saxon invaders introduced the custom of drinking it at a month-long series of festivities to celebrate a wedding—the origin of our honeymoon! The produce of the hive provided food, light, and drink in those days and in the Domesday book there are records of taxes being paid in honey and beeswax.

This country has its share of old superstitions and of legends surrounding the honey bee. These beliefs varied from one county to another, but generally speaking it has always been considered lucky when a neighbour's swarm decided to settle on your house, or in your garden. For some strange reason, it was thought unlucky to pay cash for bees, and unless they were paid for in kind, such as by the gift of eggs, fruit or other garden produce, the bees would not prosper. In the north of England, and in the midlands, it used to be the custom to make a round of the local apiaries on Christmas Eve to listen to the bees. Their buzzing was supposed to be the singing of a carol for bees have always been considered to take part in human affairs.

In fact, a Teutonic legend which is still equally strong in Britain is that the soul of man takes the form of a bee when he dies. So the bees would be offended and the honey yield poor if the bee-keeper were to die and his next of kin failed to pay a ceremonial visit to inform the bees of their sad loss.

Bees at work

Honey is a miracle food. Miraculous because it cannot be produced by man and scientists have yet to discover and understand completely the way in which bees work to produce it.

Honey has unique properties. As well as containing valuable minerals and vitamins and being a form of sugar which needs no effort to digest, pure honey will not support the growth of germs because it is hygroscopic. This means that it absorbs water and thus deprives bacteria of the essential moisture in which to multiply. Experiments have been carried out on the bacteria of many diseases whose germs have failed to survive in honey. From the earliest times its antiseptic, soothing qualities have been appreciated, and it was used as a healing dressing for wounds.

Honey contains mainly glucose and fructose, whereas household sugar is mainly sucrose. It is the action of the enzymes in the bee's honey sac which converts the sucrose in flower nectars into these other sugars, thus beginning the process of making honey. Glucose is also known as dextrose or grape sugar and fructose is frequently called levulose. Also, honey sugars being pre-digested can be absorbed by the bloodstream quickly, and thus release their energy rapidly. That is why it still plays an important role in the training diet of top athletes today, as it did in those of Ancient Greece. It has also been found effective for children with a poor appetite and frequent digestive troubles. Anaemic children respond well to a diet including plenty of honey and milk.

Every time bees go out in search of nectar, they make about 8–10 collections before returning to the hive. To collect a pound of honey, bees fly an average of 50,000 miles. About 45,000 nectar loads go into making a pound of honey. A hive of bees can store more than 2 lb. of honey a day in sunny weather.

Each hive is a most efficiently run industry, and in this industry each bee has its part to play; its own job to do. Every one works continuously and at high pressure, renouncing all individual rights in the effort to continue the colony. Some bees set out in search of the nectar flowers, or of the pollen used as protein food for the young. Other toilers have been to rivers and pools to bring back the household water supplies. As the workers arrive back, whatever their burden they are met by house bees, and these take charge of the gatherings and pack them away in the storehouse of the combs.

Other bees are preparing the cells to receive new eggs from the Queen, and some are in charge of the nurseries, feeding the young. Carpenters are building new combs, which the bees' architects and engineers have designed. Repairers, cleaners and health officers are busy keeping the hive clean, and removing the bodies of those who have worn themselves out in their labours. Some act as fanners, ceaselessly beating their wings to ventilate the hive and keep the air fresh and clean.

Also within the hive are skilful bee chemists who process the raw nectar in their expert way so that the sweetness of the flowers, the perfume, the mineral salts and other products are all preserved. Bees secrete an enzyme that converts the nectar sucrose into invert sugar (dextrose and levulose). All incoming nectar is treated in the hive, so that there are many varieties and colours of honey, each peculiar to its flower and each with its distinctive flavour.

One other and important service performed by the bees is the fertilisation of trees and plants, without which our orchards would soon cease to bear fruit.

Beekeeping as a hobby

Anyone can keep bees provided they have the interest and aptitude for it. The aptitude is most important, otherwise interest soon wanes and a most absorbing pastime fades into a painful problem.

Bees can flourish equally well in a small suburban garden as in the country. Wherever the hives are placed, however, it is most important that the bees do not become an annoyance to people and animals, and there must be room for the beekeeper to work comfortably, without being cramped for space.

The time beekeeping takes up depends very much upon the beekeeper, and the care of a single hive need not take up more than an hour or so a week. Beekeeping can be a great relaxation like gardening, only rather more adventurous, for bees do sting.

The amount of honey you can expect depends on the weather and location of the bees. Bees forage over a distance from one to one-and-a-half miles in search of food and, provided the area is not overpopulated with hives and the weather is kind, you may expect to harvest at least 40 lb. per hive.

The initial outlay to start beekeeping as a hobby is about £30, at the time of writing, but equipment can sometimes be obtained secondhand through a journal or beekeepers' club.

In choosing your site remember that bees hate wind, nor should they be exposed to a lot of sun.

If you keep bees in your garden, try to locate the hives as far away from your neighbours' boundary as possible, and handle the bees only on suitable days.

You will be most interested to watch the bees at the entrance; the pollen carriers with their great baggy 'trousers' of different coloured pollens; the nectar collectors hurrying without halt to get rid of their loads, while the guards move slowly to and fro among the frenzied fanners, examining any would-be intruder and expelling it unceremoniously. Here and there will also be seen one bee 'conversing' with another, or an entrance guard relieving a comrade of a heavy load.

Different kinds of honey

We are all becoming accustomed to the number of different honeys available, e.g. Heather honeys, Spanish Orange Blossom or Rosemary, Clover honey, Acacia honey, etc., and it is obvious from their names that the hives have been situated near a preponderance of the flower named, which will give it a particular fragrance and flavour.

The description will not be strictly accurate. The nectar from other plants can and does get mixed in a very natural way with the main bulk of the honey as it is collected by every bee in the hive. But if the main source is clover (probably about 70%) the honey will be known as Clover honey.

The various colours are a result of the different blooms from which the bees have collected the nectar. For example, honey from lime or acacia trees is pale, while that from heather is yellowy-brown and honey from woodland trees or firs is dark brown.

The fact that honey is either thick or clear is easily explained. Honey, in its natural state, at some stage becomes firm, some kinds more quickly than others—this is dependent on the amount of grape sugar contained. However, whether firm or clear, its nutritional value is the same, and honey that has become firm can easily be turned into a liquid by placing the container in hand-warm water for a time. Most people prefer set honey to use as a spread and this is produced commercially by blending honeys that have a high dextrose content at controlled temperatures to produce the firm creamy consistency we prefer.

Honey instead of sugar

Those who like honey are not always aware that it has far more uses than just as a spread on bread and butter. It can take the place of sugar entirely, but there are one or two things to remember if it is to replace sugar in cooking, especially cake-making. Honey contains 18 to 20 per cent water. Use one-fifth less than the amount stated of any liquid that is to be added, and if the recipe requires, say, 10 oz. sugar, reckon that 12 oz. honey is needed to replace it.

Choose a mild honey, such as Clover or Acacia, as a substitute for sugar in tea. Honeys with a more distinctive flavour can be used in coffee or other stronger flavoured fruit drinks, where the flavour of the honey is masked by the beverage.

The same discernment should be used when baking cakes with honey. A light coloured and delicately flavoured honey would be suitable for a Victoria Sponge, whereas a rich fruit cake could include a stronger tasting honey to improve its general flavour. One important value of honey in cake making and bread making is its moisture-retaining property, and cakes made with honey keep moist far longer than those made with sugar.

Old country recipes, of which many are given in this book, used honey because sugar was a rarity and expensive. It was also always a country housewife's choice because she was aware of its health-giving properties.

Blended honeys

Honey comes from all over the world, although the sunny countries with long summer seasons and abundant flowers produce more, because the bees can gather nectar over many months. Here in Britain we have a short summer, and uncertain weather, so we cannot produce enough honey at home to satisfy the demand. We buy honey from many countries in South America, Central Europe and the Orient. The Commonwealth, too, is a great source of supplies. Tastes in honey vary; while one person may enjoy a light coloured honey, gathered from lime flowers, another may prefer the rich, dark, almost smoky quality of pure woodland honey. Very interesting results have been obtained by blending, sometimes mixing an imported with an English honey. Some of these selected blends are sold under a brand name, ensuring an equable and high standard.

How to store honey

Store your honey in jars in a cool, dark, dry place and seal with a screw-top lid to protect from damp. Not all plastic containers are suitable for long-term storage as some are too absorbent. Label and date, as honey can be kept longer than jam and other preserves, to ensure using it up in rotation.

Recipes

Honeyed Lamb

LEG OF LAMB (3–4 LB.)
½ TEASPOON BRUISED ROSEMARY
½ OZ. MELTED BUTTER
JUICE I LARGE ORANGE
¼ TEASPOON GROUND GINGER
SALT AND PEPPER

4 TABLESPOONS CLEAR HONEY
4 TABLESPOONS RED WINE
I ORANGE, SLICED
¼ PINT BEEF STOCK
2 TEASPOONS PLAIN FLOUR

Cut small slits in the meat with a sharp knife, and insert rosemary. Place meat in a roasting tin and brush with melted butter. Pour over half the orange juice. Sprinkle meat with ginger and seasonings. Roast in a moderate oven, allowing 20–25 minutes per lb. plus 20 minutes over. After 30 minutes, pour honey over meat. Baste occasionally during cooking and, 15 minutes before meat is cooked, pour wine and remaining orange juice over it. Add orange slices to juices in roasting tin. When cooked, place lamb on serving dish. Garnish with orange slices. Blend stock gradually into flour, and stir into sauce in roasting tin. Bring to boil, stirring, cook for 1 minute, and serve with lamb.

Beef with Honey-Cherry Glaze

ROASTING JOINT OF BEEF
(2½–3 LB.)
2 TEASPOONS SUGAR
1½ OZ. BUTTER

¼ PINT BEEF STOCK
2 TABLESPOONS CHERRY JAM
I TABLESPOON CLEAR HONEY
SALT AND PEPPER

Heat the sugar with the butter. Add the meat to the pan and brown on all sides. Add the stock, reserving a tablespoon to mix with the jam and honey. Season to taste. Pour this over the meat. Roast in a moderate oven, allowing 20 minutes to the lb. and 20 minutes over, basting occasionally with the sauce.

Baked Ham with Pineapple

1 HAM OR CORNER PIECE
   GAMMON (3–4 LB.)
CLOVES

4 OZ. CLEAR HONEY
4 OZ. CRUSHED PINEAPPLE

Soak ham or gammon overnight in cold water. Drain and dry. Wrap in foil and bake in moderate oven, fat side up, allowing 30 minutes per lb. Remove foil and skin off the rind, then press cloves in about 1 inch apart over the entire surface. Add the honey to the crushed pineapple and carefully heat. Pour this syrup over the ham in a baking tin and continue baking, basting occasionally, until a rich brown glaze is obtained and the ham is tender. (Canned pineapple can be used.)

Spicy Pork Cutlets

4–6 PORK CHOPS
DRIPPING TO FRY
SALT AND PEPPER
1 TABLESPOON CLEAR HONEY

2 TABLESPOONS CRANBERRY
   JELLY
$\frac{1}{4}$ TEASPOON GROUND CLOVES

Brown pork chops quickly in hot dripping. Place in a casserole, season and cover with a mixture of honey, cranberry jelly and cloves. Cook for about 20 minutes in a moderate oven. Serve with red cabbage.

Sweet Curry

2 OZ. BUTTER
2 TABLESPOONS VEGETABLE OIL
2 LARGE ONIONS, CHOPPED
1 OZ. SEEDLESS RAISINS
1 TEASPOON CURRY SPICES
  (CLOVES, CHILLI PEPPERS, ETC.)
1 TABLESPOON CURRY POWDER
1 TEASPOON TURMERIC
1 TEASPOON PAPRIKA

1 TEASPOON SALT
2 TABLESPOONS FLOUR
4 COOKED CHICKEN PORTIONS
1 TABLESPOON SWEET CHUTNEY
2 TABLESPOONS CLEAR HONEY
2 TABLESPOONS LEMON JUICE
1 PINT STRONG CHICKEN STOCK
3 THICK SLICES FRESH PINE-
  APPLE, PEELED AND DICED

Heat the butter and oil together in a large pan. Add the onions, raisins, curry spices, and cook gently, covered, for 5 minutes. Stir in the curry powder, turmeric, paprika, salt and flour. Cook for 1 minute, add the chicken, chutney, honey, lemon juice and chicken stock. Stir well. Add the diced pineapple, cover the pan and simmer gently for about 20 minutes. Serve with fluffy boiled long grain rice and fried pappadums, or with Saffroned Rice (see following recipe).

Note: This is a very old recipe. Today it can be made with canned pineapple, and $\frac{3}{4}$ pint chicken stock made from a cube increased to 1 pint liquid with the syrup from the can.

Saffroned Rice

$\frac{1}{2}$ TEASPOON SAFFRON POWDER
$\frac{1}{2}$ TEASPOON GROUND GINGER
1 TEASPOON SALT
5 TEACUPS BOILING WATER

2 TEACUPS LONG GRAIN RICE
1 OZ. BUTTER
1 SMALL ONION, CHOPPED
1 TABLESPOON CLEAR HONEY

Steep the saffron and ground ginger in boiling water with the salt for at least 10 minutes. The water should be bright yellow and clear. In a separate pan, turn the long grain rice in the melted butter over a low heat until just transparent, stirring all the time. Add the onion to the rice, stir for a further minute, and then add the liquid. Cover the pan and simmer for about 20 minutes, or until the rice has absorbed it all and is tender. Test after about 16 minutes as rice from some parts of the world has more absorptive powers than others. Remove the pan from the heat and gently stir in the clear honey. Rice cooked in this way can be served with any other curry.

Glazed Herb Chicken

1 ROASTING CHICKEN
  (ABOUT 3½ LB.)
Stuffing :
4 OZ. SOFT BREADCRUMBS
1 OZ. ONION, MINCED OR FINELY
  CHOPPED
1 EGG
1 TABLESPOON VEGETABLE OIL

2 TEASPOONS MIXTURE THYME,
  SAGE, MARJORAM
SALT AND PEPPER
Glaze :
1½ OZ. BUTTER
3 TABLESPOONS CLEAR HONEY
½ TEASPOON MARJORAM

Wash and dry chicken. Prick with a fork and place in roasting tin. Mix stuffing ingredients well, seasoning to taste, put inside the bird. Cream butter and mix well with honey, marjoram and additional seasoning. Spread over the chicken. Bake in a moderate oven allowing 20 minutes per lb., and 20 minutes extra. Baste frequently during the cooking. Serve hot with basting sauce, or jointed cold with salad.

Chinese Duck

1 DUCK (4–4½ LB.)
2 TABLESPOONS SALT
Basting Sauce :
2 TABLESPOONS CLEAR HONEY
2 TEASPOONS WORCESTER SAUCE
1 TABLESPOON TARRAGON
  VINEGAR
½ PINT CHICKEN STOCK
Stuffing :
2 OZ. BACON, RINDED AND
  CHOPPED
1 OZ. BUTTER

2 ONIONS, SKINNED AND
  FINELY CHOPPED
2 STICKS CELERY, FINELY
  CHOPPED
4 MEDIUM COOKING APPLES,
  PEELED, CORED AND SLICED
3 OZ. SOFT BREADCRUMBS
2 TABLESPOONS CHOPPED
  PARSLEY
2 TEASPOONS CLEAR HONEY
SALT AND PEPPER

Rub salt well into the skin all over the bird. Mix basting sauce and allow to stand. Prepare stuffing: fry bacon in butter 2–3 minutes until golden brown and remove from pan. Fry onion and celery for 5 minutes and remove from pan. Fry apples 2–3 minutes. Mix all ingredients with breadcrumbs, parsley, honey and season well. Stuff the bird and truss for roasting. Put stuffed bird on a trivet, breast uppermost, and cook in a hot oven for 20 minutes. Reduce the heat to moderate. Pour basting sauce over bird and continue cooking, basting the bird every 15 minutes until cooked (about 2 hours).

Kentish Stuffed Goose

1 SMALL GOOSE
SALT
2 TABLESPOONS CLEAR HONEY
CLOVES
Stuffing :
6 OZ. PRUNES, STEWED AND STONED
12 OZ. COOKING APPLES, PEELED AND CORED
6 OZ. RICE, COOKED
2 OZ. ALMONDS, BLANCHED AND SHREDDED

SALT AND PEPPER
JUICE AND GRATED RIND $\frac{1}{2}$ LEMON
SMALL GLASS BRANDY (OPTIONAL)
1 EGG
2 TABLESPOONS CLEAR HONEY
Garnish :
CHOPPED ALMONDS
FEW COOKED CHERRIES

Rub salt on the inside of goose and smear the outside with honey, sticking a few cloves into flesh here and there. Make stuffing: cut the prunes into quarters and roughly chop the apples. Mix the fruit, rice and nuts, season to taste, add lemon rind and juice, brandy and bind together with beaten egg and honey. Stuff the bird and sew up. Roast in a moderately hot oven allowing 15 minutes per lb. and 15 minutes over. Outside should be crisp and brown. Serve the goose surrounded with the chopped almonds and cooked cherries. The same recipe is excellent using cooked halved and stoned apricots instead of the cherries.

Basted Chicken

1 FRYING CHICKEN
1 EGG
2 TABLESPOONS VEGETABLE OIL
2 TEASPOONS WORCESTER SAUCE

2 OZ. CLEAR HONEY
2 TABLESPOONS LEMON JUICE
2 TEASPOONS PAPRIKA
1 TEASPOON SALT

Cut the chicken into serving-sized portions, arrange in a greased baking dish. Beat egg, add remaining ingredients, mix well. Spoon mixture over chicken pieces, place in a moderate oven for 1 hour. Turn and baste the chicken pieces frequently with the honey sauce while it is cooking. Increase the oven heat for the last 10 minutes to give pieces a crisp brown skin.

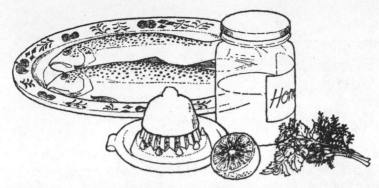

Lime Marinade for fish

I SMALL ONION, CHOPPED
2 LIMES OR LEMONS
2 TABLESPOONS OLIVE OIL
I TEASPOON CLEAR HONEY

3 TEASPOONS CHOPPED FRESH
  HERBS
¼ TEASPOON TABASCO SAUCE

Mix the finely chopped onion with the juice of the limes or lemons and the other ingredients. Lay thick fillets or small whole fish in the marinade overnight or for several hours before cooking.

Cider Marinade for chicken, veal or ham

¼ PINT CIDER
4 TABLESPOONS HONEY
GOOD PINCH NUTMEG

4 TABLESPOONS LEMON JUICE OR
  WHITE WINE VINEGAR
SOFT BROWN SUGAR

Mix together the cider, honey, nutmeg and lemon juice or vinegar. Pour over the chicken or meat, before roasting. Sprinkle lightly with sugar. Baste during roasting with the juices in the pan.

Mustard Marinade for meat

2 TABLESPOONS CLEAR HONEY
2 TEASPOONS FRENCH MUSTARD
I TABLESPOON VEGETABLE OIL
½ PINT ORANGE JUICE
2 TABLESPOONS LEMON JUICE

¼ PINT TOMATO KETCHUP
½ TEASPOON GROUND GINGER
GOOD PINCH CAYENNE PEPPER
SALT TO TASTE

Bring the first 6 ingredients to the boil and simmer very gently until slightly thickened. Season with remaining ingredients, cook for a few more minutes, then cool. Use to marinade before cooking.

31

Vegetables

Beans baked with honey

I LB. DRIED HARICOT BEANS
½ TEASPOON BICARBONATE OF
    SODA
2 TABLESPOONS OLIVE OIL
I LARGE ONION, CHOPPED

3–4 SLICES FAT BACON, DICED
8 OZ. TOMATOES, QUARTERED
I TEASPOON FRENCH MUSTARD
4 OZ. CLEAR HONEY
2 TABLESPOONS TOMATO PURÉE

Soak haricots overnight in water with bicarbonate of soda. Cook in salted water until just tender, drain, put into a greased casserole. Heat half the oil in a pan and lightly fry onion and diced bacon. Pour contents of pan into casserole, add tomatoes, mustard, remaining oil, honey and tomato purée. Mix and bake in a moderate oven for 1 hour.

Onions with Honey Sauce

I½ LB. MEDIUM SIZED ONIONS
½ PINT WINE AND WATER MIXED
Sauce :
2 TEASPOONS CORNFLOUR

I TEASPOON CLEAR HONEY
PINCH MARJORAM
JUICE ½ LEMON
SALT AND PEPPER

Skin onions and cook gently until tender in the wine mixture. Take out and keep warm. Make the sauce by mixing cornflour, honey, marjoram, lemon juice and seasoning to taste to a smooth paste. Add to liquid used for cooking onions, bring to boil, stirring. Quarter the onions and cover with the sauce.

Bacon Potatoes

2 LB. POTATOES, BOILED IN
    SKINS
I OZ. BUTTER
2 OZ. WHOLEMEAL FLOUR
½ PINT STOCK
4 OZ. FINELY CHOPPED BACON

2 TABLESPOONS MUSTARD
I TABLESPOON CLEAR HONEY
I GLASS RED WINE
SALT, CAYENNE PEPPER, CURRY
    POWDER
¼ PINT CREAM

Skin and slice the potatoes and put into fireproof dish. Melt the butter in a saucepan and cook the flour in it for 2 minutes, stirring. Add the stock and the bacon, then the mustard mixed with honey, and the wine. Season with salt, cayenne and a little curry powder.

Bring to the boil, stirring. Cook until smooth. Pour over the potatoes and heat in a moderate oven for 20 minutes. Add the cream and serve.

Bramble Salad

1 LB. DESSERT APPLES	3 TABLESPOONS VEGETABLE OIL
2 TABLESPOONS LEMON JUICE	1 TABLESPOON CLEAR HONEY
8 OZ. BLACKBERRIES	1 TABLESPOON FRESH MINT,
2 TABLESPOONS WHITE WINE	CHOPPED
VINEGAR	SALT AND PEPPER TO TASTE

Peel, core and thinly slice apples into lemon juice to prevent them from discolouring. Prepare blackberries and add to the apples. Beat together vinegar, oil, honey, mint and seasonings. Pour over the salad.

CAKES AND BISCUITS

Honey Gingerbread

8 OZ. BUTTER OR MARGARINE	8 OZ. SEEDLESS RAISINS
8 OZ. MOIST BROWN SUGAR	*Topping :*
$\frac{1}{2}$ PINT MILK	2 OZ. CHOPPED WALNUTS
$\frac{1}{4}$ LB. BLACK TREACLE	4 TABLESPOONS CLEAR HONEY
4 TABLESPOONS CLEAR HONEY	$1\frac{1}{2}$ OZ. BROWN SUGAR
2 EGGS	2 OZ. BUTTER OR MARGARINE
1 LB. PLAIN FLOUR	(MELTED)
1 TEASPOON GROUND GINGER	$\frac{1}{2}$ TEASPOON CINNAMON
1 TEASPOON BICARBONATE OF SODA	

Cream butter and sugar until light and fluffy. Add warmed milk, treacle and honey. Beat the eggs and add to the mixture. Sieve together the dry ingredients and beat well into the mixture until smooth. Stir in the raisins. Pour into a greased and bottom-lined cake tin, either round or square, and bake in a slow oven for $2\frac{1}{4}$ hours or until firm to the touch. To make the topping, blend ingredients together. Remove cake from oven and whilst hot spread with topping. Brown under grill for 2–3 minutes. Allow to cool before removing cake from tin.

Variation: Different toppings can be used. Melt 2 tablespoons of finely cut marmalade and spread over the top of the cake while it is still warm, or allow to get cold and coat with glacé icing.

Honey-Nut Puff

8 OZ. PUFF PASTRY
Filling :
5 OZ. GRATED HAZEL AND
   WALNUTS

2 TABLESPOONS SUGAR
2 OZ. FINE BISCUIT CRUMBS
2 TABLESPOONS HONEY
MILK TO MIX

Roll out the pastry thinly and spread with the filling made by heating the nuts, sugar, crumbs and honey in a little milk until blended. Leave it to cool. Roll the pastry up with filling inside, moisten and seal the ends. It can be twisted into a crescent or left as a roll. Brush with beaten egg and bake in a hot oven for 20–25 minutes, until light golden.

Honey and Spice Banana Loaf

6 OZ. SELF-RAISING FLOUR
1 TEASPOON SALT
1 TEASPOON MIXED SPICE
2 OZ. SOFT BROWN SUGAR
1½ OZ. WALNUTS, CHOPPED

2 RIPE BANANAS
3 OZ. CLEAR HONEY
1 EGG, WELL BEATEN
1 OZ. BUTTER OR MARGARINE,
   MELTED

Grease and line bottom of a 1-lb. loaf tin. Sift flour, salt and spice together. Stir in sugar and chopped walnuts. Mash the bananas and add to flour mixture with honey, beaten egg and melted fat, stirring until well blended. Turn into prepared tin and bake in a moderate oven for 1 hour. Remove from tin, cool on a wire tray.

Cobble Cakes

4½ OZ. CLEAR HONEY
2 OZ. BUTTER
2 OZ. SUGAR
1 OZ. GROUND ALMONDS
1 OZ. CHOPPED CANDIED PEEL
1 EGG
½ TEASPOON GROUND CINNAMON
GROUND CLOVES, GINGER
1 TABLESPOON RUM

7 OZ. PLAIN FLOUR
2 OZ. CORNFLOUR
2 TEASPOONS BAKING POWDER
Icing :
4½ OZ. ICING SUGAR, SIEVED
GRATED ZEST 1 LEMON
1 TEASPOON VANILLA
   ESSENCE

Heat the honey with the butter and sugar until it melts; do not boil. Beat together the almonds, peel, egg and cinnamon. Add ground cloves and ginger according to taste, and the rum. Sift together the flour, cornflour and baking powder, and knead together with the other ingredients. Shape the dough into a roll, cut into slices and put on a greased baking tray. Bake in a hot oven for 20 minutes. Beat up the icing sugar, and lemon zest with the vanilla essence and spread on the slices when cool.

Honey Almond Dessert Cake

4 OZ. BUTTER OR MARGARINE	*Topping and filling :*
2 OZ. SOFT BROWN SUGAR	3 OZ. BUTTER
2 TABLESPOONS THICK HONEY	1½ TABLESPOONS THICK HONEY
2 EGGS, BEATEN	3 OZ. ICING SUGAR, SIEVED
6 OZ. SELF-RAISING FLOUR	1½ OZ. FLAKED, TOASTED
4 TABLESPOONS MILK	ALMONDS

Grease and line a 7-inch cake tin. Cream butter, sugar and honey together until light and creamy. Beat in blended eggs, a little at a time, adding a little flour with the last amount of egg. Fold in remaining flour and milk. Pour into tin and bake in a moderate oven for 45 minutes. Cool on a wire tray. To make filling, soften butter and beat in honey and icing sugar till light and creamy. Split cake and sandwich together with one-third of butter cream. Cover top and sides with remainder. Scatter top and sides with flaked almonds.

Banbury Cakes

4 OZ. BUTTER	8 OZ. CURRANTS
1 TABLESPOON CLEAR HONEY	½ OZ. ALLSPICE
4 OZ. CANDIED LEMON PEEL	GOOD PINCH CINNAMON
2 OZ. CANDIED ORANGE PEEL	1 LB. FLAKY PASTRY

Cream the butter with the honey, stir in the candied peel, currants and spices. Roll out the pastry thinly, cut into 4-inch or 6-inch squares. Put a tablespoonful of mixture in the centre of each square. Fold edges in to the middle, form into a round or oval shape, turn over and roll lightly to flatten. Cut 3 small slits across the top, bake in a moderately hot oven on an ungreased baking sheet for 25 minutes.

Note: Eccles cakes are similar, with a slightly more solid filling, and are usually brushed with lightly beaten white of egg and caster sugar before baking. Coventry Godcakes are the same, except that the square of pastry is folding diagonally over the filling to make a triangle, and these are always sold at Easter. The three slashes, and the three-cornered shape of the Godcakes symbolise the Trinity.

Honey Scrunchies

2 OZ. BUTTER	4 OZ. PLAIN FLOUR
I OZ. SUGAR	I OZ. ROLLED OATS
1½ OZ. CLEAR HONEY	½ TEASPOON BICARBONATE OF SODA

Heat the butter, sugar and honey together in a saucepan. Mix the flour, rolled oats and bicarbonate of soda together in a bowl. Add the honey mixture to the dry ingredients and mix well with a wooden spoon. Form by hand into small balls the size of a walnut, flatten slightly and place on a baking sheet, well apart to allow them to spread. Bake in a preheated moderate oven for 15–20 minutes, until golden brown. Cool on a wire tray. If liked, press half a glacé cherry or half a walnut into the flattened balls of biscuit dough before baking.

Chocolate Cake with Orange Frosting

4 OZ. SELF-RAISING FLOUR	*Icing :*
I OZ. GROUND RICE	4 OZ. BUTTER, SOFTENED
4 OZ. PLAIN CHOCOLATE, GRATED	6 OZ. ICING SUGAR, SIEVED
4 OZ. BUTTER	I TABLESPOON CLEAR HONEY
2 OZ. CASTER SUGAR	GRATED ZEST I ORANGE
2 TABLESPOONS CLEAR HONEY	I TABLESPOON MILK
I–2 TEASPOONS VANILLA ESSENCE	ORANGE FOOD COLOURING
2 EGGS, BEATEN	I OZ. GRATED CHOCOLATE

Grease and line a 6-inch cake tin. Sieve together the flour and ground rice. Melt the chocolate in a basin over hot water. Cream the butter, sugar, honey and essence until pale and fluffy. Add the melted chocolate and mix lightly together. Beat in the egg a little at a time. Fold in the flour, turn mixture into the tin and bake in a moderate oven for 1–1½ hours. Make icing by creaming butter and sugar together until light and fluffy. Beat in honey and orange zest, add milk and a few drops of colouring. Mix well. Spread icing over cake, making soft peaks. Sprinkle with grated chocolate.

Chocolate Icing

6 OZ. UNSWEETENED CHOCOLATE 8 OZ. ICING SUGAR, SIEVED
4 TABLESPOONS CLEAR HONEY 2 TABLESPOONS WARM WATER

Melt chocolate and honey in a basin over hot water. Cool. Beat in half the sugar, stir in water and remaining sugar and beat well. Can be used inside cake and for coating top and sides.

Coffee Fudge Icing

6 OZ. ICING SUGAR I TABLESPOON MILK
2 OZ. MARGARINE, CUT UP FINELY 2-3 TEASPOONS COFFEE
3 TEASPOONS CLEAR HONEY ESSENCE

Sift the icing sugar into a bowl. Put the fat, honey, milk and essence into a small saucepan. Stir over a gentle heat till hot but not boiling and until the fat has melted. Pour at once into the icing sugar and stir mixture with a wooden spoon until smooth. Add a few drops of hot water if too thick.

Lemon Nut Filling

2 OZ. BUTTER 2 OZ. CLEAR HONEY
8 OZ. ICING SUGAR 2 OZ. CHOPPED WALNUTS
2 TEASPOONS LEMON JUICE

Beat butter until soft and gradually beat in sifted icing sugar, lemon juice and honey. Add chopped nuts.

Honey Meringue

I EGG WHITE 4 OZ. CLEAR HONEY

Beat egg white until stiff. Then add honey, beating until meringue stands in peaks. Use on puddings or cakes.

Ginger Snaps

Heat together 8 oz. honey, ½ oz. butter and ¼ oz. ground ginger. When nearly cold stir in enough flour to thicken. Roll out thinly, cut into small rounds, and bake on a greased tray for 15 minutes. Cool on wire tray and store in airtight container. (The unbaked biscuit dough can be wrapped in foil and frozen.)

Brandy Snaps

3½ OZ. PLAIN FLOUR   6 OZ. CLEAR HONEY
3 OZ. CASTER SUGAR   4 OZ. BUTTER OR MARGARINE
I TEASPOON CINNAMON

Sieve the flour into the sugar and cinnamon. Heat honey just to
boiling point. Stir in butter. Add the flour mixture and mix well.
Drop ½ teaspoon portions of the mixture on to greased baking
sheets allowing room for spreading. Bake in a preheated slow oven
for 15–18 minutes. Remove from oven and cool for 2 minutes.
Lift them carefully from the tin one at a time. Quickly roll each
around the greased handle of a wooden spoon. Place on a cooling
rack to harden. If they become too brittle for shaping, replace in
oven for 1 minute to reheat, then roll. Store in an airtight tin.

When I was a child these were served on special occasions filled
with whipped cream. At Christmas time, the cream was flavoured
with brandy and sweetened with icing sugar.

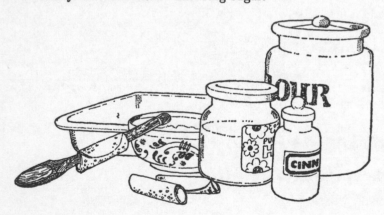

Christmas Tree Biscuits

I LB. SELF-RAISING FLOUR   6 OZ. BUTTER OR MARGARINE
½ TEASPOON CINNAMON   7 TABLESPOONS CLEAR HONEY
¼ TEASPOON GINGER   *To decorate :*
I TEASPOON GRATED LEMON   A LITTLE GLACÉ ICING
  RIND

Sieve dry ingredients together, add lemon rind and rub in butter
until mixture resembles fine breadcrumbs. Melt honey over a

gentle heat and pour into the mixture. Work in by hand until a dough is formed. Knead lightly on a floured board and roll out thinly. Cut out fancy shapes and put on a greased baking sheet. Make a small hole near the top of each shape with a small cutter. Bake in a very slow oven for 20–25 minutes. Cool on wire tray. Outline or decorate with glacé icing. Thread ribbon through the holes to hang on the tree.

SWEETS AND DESSERTS

Honey Fruit Dish

$\frac{1}{4}$ PINT GRAPE JUICE
1 TABLESPOON CLEAR HONEY
1 TABLESPOON CREAM
1 APPLE

1 ORANGE
1 BANANA
8 HAZELNUTS, GRATED

Mix the juice and honey with the cream. Soak the peeled and sliced apple, orange and banana in this mixture and sprinkle the nuts over the fruit.

Gingered Pear Salad

4 DESSERT PEARS
2 TABLESPOONS LEMON JUICE
1 TABLESPOON PRESERVED
  GINGER
2 TABLESPOONS GINGER SYRUP

JUICE 1 LARGE ORANGE
2 TEASPOONS BRANDY
1 TABLESPOON CLEAR HONEY
8 GLACÉ CHERRIES, CHOPPED

Peel, core and slice the pears into lemon juice to prevent them from discolouring. Mix the finely chopped preserved ginger, syrup, orange juice, brandy and honey. Pour the mixture over the pears and stir gently. Serve in small glass dishes garnished with cherries.

Grilled Grapefruit

1 LARGE GRAPEFRUIT
1 TABLESPOON CLEAR HONEY

2 TEASPOONS DEMERARA SUGAR
2 MARASCHINO CHERRIES

Halve the grapefruit. Loosen sections and remove core and pips if any. Spread honey over. Sprinkle with the sugar. Grill until sugar melts and surface is bubbly and golden. Decorate with a cherry. Serve as a meal starter or dessert. (Serves 2.)

Cherry Peach Cream

4 LARGE FRESH PEACHES, PEELED
SMALL BOTTLE MARASCHINO
   CHERRIES
3 EGG YOLKS

6 TABLESPOONS CLEAR HONEY
2 EGG WHITES
1 PINT MILK

Halve the peaches and place 2 halves in each of 4 sundae glasses. Sprinkle each with a teaspoon of the cherry juice. Beat together the egg yolks and the honey, and fold in the stiffly beaten whites. Heat the milk, but do not boil, and then quickly beat into the mixture. Place the bowl over pan of hot water and continue to beat until the cream thickens. Do not cook it over direct heat. Pour the cooled cream over the peaches. Decorate each portion with 3 cherries.

Banana Delight

1 LB. BANANAS (WEIGHT
   WITHOUT SKIN)
¾ PINT MILK
2 TABLESPOONS ORANGE JUICE

3 TABLESPOONS CLEAR HONEY
PINCH SALT
4 TEASPOONS GELATINE
¼ PINT HOT WATER

Mash bananas until smooth. Add milk, orange juice, honey and salt. Stir in gelatine, dissolved in hot water. Pour into a basin. When set, serve plain or with whipped cream lightly sprinkled with cinnamon.

Pickwick Pudding

8 OZ. BUTTER
4 OZ. BROWN SUGAR
4 OZ. HONEY
4 EGGS
4 OZ. PLAIN FLOUR
½ TEASPOON NUTMEG
½ TEASPOON MIXED SPICE

8 OZ. SOFT BREADCRUMBS
1 LB. SULTANAS
1 LB. RAISINS
2 OZ. CHOPPED CANDIED PEEL
2 OZ. BLANCHED, CHOPPED
   ALMONDS
1 TABLESPOON BRANDY

Cream butter, sugar and honey together, add the eggs one at a time, and beat well. Add sifted flour and spices, then the breadcrumbs, fruit and nuts. Now add the brandy. Place in a well-greased basin, cover with greaseproof paper and cloth and steam for at least 5 hours. This pudding improves with keeping.

Lattice Apple Tart

9 OZ. FLOUR
PINCH SALT
4½ OZ. BUTTER
2 EGG YOLKS
2 TABLESPOONS CREAM
Filling :
1 LB. 4 OZ. APPLES

3 OZ. BUTTER
2½ OZ. SUGAR
GRATED ZEST 1 ORANGE
1 TEASPOON CINNAMON
1 PINT DRY CIDER
CLEAR HONEY

Make a short pastry by rubbing the flour, salt and butter and mixing in the beaten egg yolks and cream. Roll out and line a tart plate or dish, keeping enough for lattice strips. Cook 'blind' for 10 minutes in a hot oven. Allow to cool and cover with the filling made by cooking the sliced apples, butter, sugar, orange zest and cinnamon in the cider. When cool place on pastry and thickly coat with honey. Using the remains of the pastry, arrange strips over the tart in a lattice design. Cook for 20–25 minutes in a moderate oven.

Bread and Butter Pudding

6 THIN SLICES OF BREAD
1 OZ. BUTTER
2 TABLESPOONS SULTANAS
2 EGGS

1 TABLESPOON HONEY
1 PINT MILK
GRATED NUTMEG

Butter the bread and cut into squares. Build it up in layers in a fireproof dish with fruit sprinkled in between. Beat eggs and honey, add milk and mix well. Pour over the bread. Grate nutmeg on top. Stand dish in a larger dish with water. Bake in a very slow oven until set: 30–40 minutes.

Honey Junket

4 TEASPOONS CLEAR HONEY
1 PINT MILK
2–3 DROPS VANILLA ESSENCE

3 TEASPOONS ESSENCE OF
RENNET

Warm honey over a gentle heat until runny. Add milk and vanilla and stir until lukewarm. Stir in the rennet. Pour at once into bowl or individual dishes. Leave to set and then chill. (Children like this with cherries or plums stewed with rose syrup.)

Honey Ice Cream

½ PINT DOUBLE CREAM	4 OZ. CHOPPED DATES
8 OZ. CLEAR HONEY	4 OZ. CHOPPED FIGS
2 OZ. GLACÉ CHERRIES	2 OZ. CHOPPED PISTACHIO NUTS

Beat up the cream with the honey. Stir in the cherries, dates, figs and pistachio nuts. Pack into a dish and freeze solid in the refrigerator. The texture is improved if the mixture is beaten again well when half frozen and returned to the freezing dish.

Hazelnut Honey Balls

2 OZ. GRATED HAZELNUTS	2 TABLESPOONS CLEAR HONEY
1 OZ. GRATED CHOCOLATE	1 TEASPOON VANILLA ESSENCE
1½ OZ. SUGAR	FINELY CHOPPED ALMONDS
GRATED PEEL ½ LEMON	

Mix together the nuts, chocolate, sugar, lemon peel, honey and vanilla essence. With damp hands make ten balls from this mixture and roll them in finely chopped almonds. Put on a baking sheet to dry out and set. Store in an airtight container.

Honey Toffee

2 TABLESPOONS BUTTER	1 LB. SOFT BROWN SUGAR
1 LB. CLEAR HONEY	

Melt butter in a large pan. Add honey and sugar, stir gently to dissolve, and boil 10 minutes or until a few drops set crisp when tested in cold water. Turn into a greased dish and cut into squares just before it sets hard. Wrap in waxed paper.

Honey Marshmallows

1 TABLESPOON GELATINE	8 OZ. CLEAR HONEY
6 TABLESPOONS COLD WATER	12 OZ. DESICCATED COCONUT

Soak gelatine in cold water, then dissolve over hot water and add to warmed honey. Beat about 20 minutes till light and fluffy. Turn out on to oiled sandwich tin and leave to stand 48 hours. Toast the coconut, spread it over the surface of a large tin and turn marshmallow on to it. Dip a knife in cold water and cut into squares. Roll each piece in coconut.

Honey Butter

8 OZ. FRESH BUTTER   I TEASPOON LEMON JUICE
6 TEASPOONS CLEAR HONEY   PINCH GINGER

Mix the butter with the honey and add the lemon juice and ginger, mix thoroughly. Makes a sandwich filling or spread.

Honey Cheese Spread

4 OZ. CREAM CHEESE   I OZ. SULTANAS
2 TABLESPOONS CLEAR HONEY

Cream cheese and honey together until smooth. Stir in sultanas. Use as a filling for a cake or as a spread on bread and biscuits.

SAUCES AND DRESSINGS

Chocolate Fudge Sauce

4 TABLESPOONS CLEAR HONEY   4 OZ. PLAIN CHOCOLATE

Warm the honey until hot but not boiling. Take off the heat. Stir in the broken-up chocolate until dissolved. Use lukewarm to pour over ice cream.

Apple Sauce

8 OZ. UNSWEETENED APPLE   I TABLESPOON LEMON JUICE
    PURÉE   I TABLESPOON CLEAR HONEY

Put all ingredients into a small saucepan, and heat gently for a few minutes. Serve with sweets or savoury dishes such as lamb or pork.

Lemon Sauce

6 TABLESPOONS WATER   GRATED ZEST $\frac{1}{2}$ LEMON
2 TEASPOONS ARROWROOT   I TABLESPOON LEMON JUICE
3 TABLESPOONS THICK HONEY

Blend 2 teaspoons water with the arrowroot. Stir in the remainder of the water. Pour into saucepan with honey, lemon zest and juice, and cook, stirring until it thickens. Serve with steamed puddings or pour lukewarm over vanilla ice cream.

Cereal Sauce

½ PINT MILK
1 TABLESPOON HONEY

¼ TEASPOON CINNAMON

Warm milk with honey until honey dissolves in milk. Add cinnamon and whisk well until frothy. Use for pouring over porridge or cereals.

Honey Mayonnaise

1 WHOLE EGG OR 2 YOLKS
1 TEASPOON SALT
1 TEASPOON MADE MUSTARD
1 TABLESPOON HONEY
1 TEASPOON WHITE WINE VINEGAR

2 TABLESPOONS LEMON JUICE
GOOD PINCH PEPPER
SMALL PINCH CAYENNE
¼–½ PINT SALAD OIL

Put the egg or yolks into a bowl or blender, with the salt, mustard, honey, a few drops of the vinegar, and of the lemon juice. Season to taste with the peppers. Whisk or blend thoroughly, then start beating in the oil. When half has been added, put in the rest of the vinegar and lemon juice, and continue whisking or blending in oil until the mayonnaise is the consistency of lightly whipped double cream.

Honey Salad Dressing

½ PINT SALAD OIL
¼ PINT CIDER VINEGAR
3 TABLESPOONS CLEAR HONEY

½ TEASPOON BLACK PEPPER
½ TEASPOON PAPRIKA PEPPER
½ TEASPOON SALT

Put all ingredients into a large jar with screw on lid, and shake well. Use when required.

Creamed Horse-radish

1 TABLESPOON CLEAR HONEY
½ PINT DOUBLE CREAM

5 TABLESPOONS GRATED
  HORSE-RADISH
1 COOKING APPLE

Beat up the honey with the cream, and add the horse-radish. Grate the apple and add to the mixture. Allow at least 1 hour for flavour to develop before serving. The sauce tends to discolour if kept uncovered. Serve with hot or cold roast beef.

Cucumber Cream

1 FRESH CUCUMBER
1 CARTON YOGURT
½ TEASPOON SEA SALT AND
  BLACK PEPPER, MIXED

2 SPRIGS PARSLEY
2 TEASPOONS CLEAR HONEY
1 CRUSHED CLOVE GARLIC

Wash cucumber, dry and cut into very thin slices unpeeled. Let them stand for several minutes in salt water, then dry well. Empty the chilled yogurt into a dish and add the salt and pepper, cucumber slices, chopped parsley, honey and garlic. Beat the mixture to a smooth cream with a wooden spoon, or liquidiser. Serve ice-cold with toast, or with meat or fish.

DRINKS

Vin Chaud or Hot Honey Punch

1 BOTTLE RED WINE
3 TABLESPOONS CLEAR HONEY
GOOD PINCH CINNAMON

1 ORANGE, STUDDED WITH
  CLOVES
1 PINT BOILING WATER
1 MINIATURE BOTTLE BRANDY

Heat wine, honey and cinnamon with the orange. Stir well. Add boiling water and just before serving pour in the brandy. For a more pungent drink substitute a lemon for the orange, and a little freshly grated nutmeg may replace the cinnamon.

Hot Honeyed Orange

6 ORANGES
3 LEMONS
½ PINT WATER

9 TABLESPOONS CLEAR HONEY
CLOVES

Squeeze the juice from 5 oranges and 3 lemons. Add water and sweeten with honey. Heat until almost boiling. Pour into mugs. Slice the remaining orange and press one or two cloves into the centre of each slice. Float an orange slice on the top of each mug.

Vicar's Prune Tea

8 OZ. PRUNES
8 OZ. CLEAR HONEY
JUICE 4 LARGE LEMONS

JUICE 4 LARGE ORANGES
½ PINT STRONG TEA
(STRAINED AND CHILLED)

Put the prunes to soak overnight in a saucepan with the honey and sufficient water to cover them well. Bring slowly to the boil and simmer until the prunes are just cooked. Drain through a sieve and add the fruit juices and tea to the syrup in the pan. Chill the mixture well, and serve in glasses. The prunes can be served with cereal for breakfast.

Mint Cooler

4 TABLESPOONS CLEAR HONEY
4 OZ. SUGAR
12 CRUSHED MINT LEAVES

¼ PINT WATER
4 LEMONS
4 SPRIGS MINT

Boil honey, sugar, crushed mint leaves and water together for 4 minutes. Add juice of three lemons, strain. One-third fill glasses with this syrup. Fill up with crushed ice and chilled tonic water. Float slice of lemon and mint sprig on top. Dry ginger or sparkling lemonade can replace tonic water.

Orange Yogurt Refresher

1 CARTON YOGURT
1 ORANGE

2 TEASPOONS CLEAR HONEY

Whisk up yogurt, add orange juice and honey and whisk until blended. Otherwise yogurt, peeled and quartered orange and honey can be whipped up in a liquidiser.

Yogurt Dressing

5 OZ. CARTON NATURAL YOGURT   1 TABLESPOON CLEAR HONEY
2 TABLESPOONS LEMON JUICE   SALT AND PEPPER TO TASTE

Put all ingredients into a basin. Mix together well with a wooden spoon. Serve with hard-boiled egg salad, potato salad, raw vegetable salads.

Honey Lemonade

1 LB. CLEAR HONEY   MINERAL WATER
JUICE 3 LEMONS

Mix the honey with the lemon juice. For every 1½ oz. add one small bottle of mineral water. Whisk until well blended.

Household Uses

Honey is a natural bactericide: These recipes are based on old country cures and hints, which were found remarkably effective in the days when housewives had no chemist's shop and possibly even no doctor to consult.

Honey Posset: Bring 1 pint of milk almost to the boil. Add 2 tablespoons honey, the juice of 1 lemon and boil slowly until the curd separates. An old country dish for invalids.

Lemon and Honey Cordial: Mix juice of half a lemon with 1 tablespoon honey in a tumbler, and fill up with hot water. Useful for sore throats and inducing sleep.

Granny Creasey's Cough Cure: Peel and chop finely 1 lb. onions. Add 2 oz. honey, 12 oz. brown sugar and 2 pints of water. Simmer gently over a low heat for 3 hours. When mixture is cool, bottle and cork it well. This keeps over the winter. Take 4–6 tablespoons a day; excellent for hoarseness and to alleviate whooping cough.

Strong Cough Mixture: Mix together 4 oz. honey, 4 oz. treacle and 5 fluid oz. white wine vinegar and simmer over a low heat for 15 minutes. Bottle and cork firmly when cold.

Mild Cough Mixture: Mix 6 oz. clear honey with 2 oz. glycerine and the juice of 2 lemons. Stir well. Bottle and cork.

Hay Fever: Sufferers are recommended to chew honey-comb cappings 3–4 times during the day when the pollen count is high; if these are not available 2 teaspoons of clear honey at each meal will achieve some relief.

Invalid's Tonic: Place the finely grated rind of a lemon in a third of a pint of milk and bring to the boil. Strain the liquid through a sieve. Beat 2 egg yolks with 2 tablespoons honey and carefully blend into the warm milk. Add 3 tablespoons of brandy.

King Hal's Nightcap: Bring to the boil 1 pint brown ale, a good pinch of allspice, 2 cloves and 2 tablespoons of clear honey. Drink hot. Not necessarily a soporific!

Scalds: There are many testimonies to the healing properties of honey applied to scalds. Poured on to a clean dressing and applied to the scald, it will relieve pain and promote quick healing.

Flesh wounds: Especially where the injury has become septic, applications of honey cleanse and heal.

A persistent festering: Honey will draw out the poisons causing the swelling and help form new healthy tissues.

Carpenter's Cure: Until modern times, the quick treatment in the building trade for a deep cut was a compound of honey and cobwebs. The cobwebs, even if dusty, were applied first to stop the bleeding then, later, the cuts smeared over with honey and tightly bound up. Carpenters were particularly liable to deep cuts, hence the name.

Chickenpox spots: These can be treated with honey to reduce itching, and heal sooner without leaving scars. All irritating skin rashes are soothed by applying honey frequently.

For chapped or roughened hands: Put 6 oz. honey, $4\frac{1}{2}$ oz. clean beeswax and 6 oz. lard into a double saucepan. Melt all together, stirring, remove from heat and continue to stir until cool. Then add 2 drams each of attar of bergamot and attar of cloves. Keep in cold-cream jars.

Skin discolouration: This can be remedied by a mixture of honey and the juice of watercress. Spread on the face, leave to dry and wash off after 1 to 2 hours. Repeat daily, until skin is clear.

To treat freckles: Stir crushed fennel seeds into warmed, clear honey until of a thick consistency. Spread on the face and leave for 15 minutes. Wash off with warm water. Also effective for brown spots and wrinkles.

A simple facial: Blend $2\frac{1}{2}$ oz. finely ground oatmeal with 3 teaspoons clear honey (a little more if necessary to achieve a paste). Lastly, blend in 1 teaspoon rose water. To use; spread the paste evenly over the face after first having cleansed it with water. Relax quietly for a good half-hour. Rinse in cold water and pat with witch hazel. Good for softening a weathered skin.

Refresher for dry skins: Beat together 3 teaspoons of fresh linseed oil and 1 egg yolk. Add 1 teaspoon honey. Mix well. Spread on the skin with a soft brush and leave for 15 minutes. Wash off with rose water.

49

Compress for tired eyes: Mix a half tablespoon honey in about ¼ pint strong camomile infusion. Soak compresses in this mixture and place for 30 minutes on the closed eyes.

Treatment for dry hair: This treatment is not suitable for blonde hair as it tends to darken the colour slightly. Add 3 oz. clear honey to 2 fluid oz. olive oil. Shake together in a bottle, cork well, and store for up to 4 weeks. To use, shake the bottle and massage the mixture into the roots of the hair at least half an hour before applying a mild shampoo to wash it off.

Using beeswax

Dressing for a sprain: Take equal parts of glycerine and castor oil; and add to them a little beeswax which has been melted in readiness. Mix well together. This is a simple and soothing unguent applied on a pad and tightly bandaged in place.

Farmhouse furniture wax: Shred 2 oz. beeswax, 1 oz. white wax, 2 squares of camphor into ½ pint turpentine. Shred 1 oz. Castile soap and simmer it in ½ pint soft water until the quantity is reduced to half. Let it cool a little. Now mix all together and add 1 teaspoon of ammonia; take care to keep well away from the eyes when adding this. Put into a jar with a firm lid, and shake well before use.

To strengthen sewing thread: Make a small block of beeswax to keep in the sewing basket. Pass the thread over it to coat with wax before sewing on buttons. A disc of wax with a hole in the centre can be hung on the sewing machine so that the thread passes through it.

Sealing jars and bottles: A thin layer of melted beeswax is an effective way of sealing bottled fruits, vegetables and preserves.

HERBS

Herbal lore and legends associated with herbs have been part of man's heritage since time began. Before the age of physicians, people developed the same instinct as animals living in the wild for recognising the plants which were safe and good to eat.

All through history there have been stories of gardens—from the days of the Garden of Eden. There was the famous garden of Lucullus, in Rome. Then later, the herb or 'physic' gardens of the medieval monasteries, where monks grew herbs to cure the sick. Our first drugs were dried medicinal plants, the name being derived from the Saxon word *dregen*, to dry.

We owe most of our cooking traditions to the Romans, who when they came to Britain brought with them about four hundred different herbs for both culinary and medicinal use. King Alfred's favourite book mentioned five hundred known varieties of his time. The Romans in turn owed their knowledge of herbal arts to the Indians, Egyptians and Greeks. Among the herbs they brought with them were many we use today, such as chervil, lovage, parsley, sage and thyme. After the Romans left, many herbs naturalised, although no longer cultivated during the subsequent Dark Ages.

These herbs would, if they had gone out of use, have been reintroduced by the Normans, more sophisticated mainland Europeans than the backward islanders of Britain. We know herbs were extensively cultivated by our monks from the early Middle Ages, and became an important item in the still-room of the old manor house and castle. They were precious medicines, flavourings and preservatives.

From fifteenth-century records, it is obvious that an important use for herbs was to disguise the fact that meat was 'high' during summer and rather over-salty in winter, because it had to be salted in order to keep it.

Spices, of course, were used for the same purpose. A nosegay of flowers and sweet herbs, such as the Judge found it advisable to hold between himself and the vulgar prisoner at the bar was an example, as was the pomander (an orange stuck with cloves and rolled in orris root and cinnamon when dry) for scenting linen. Spices, particularly the peppery varieties, preserved meat, and disguised its age. But it is interesting to note that in old country recipes herbs, which grew freely in the garden, were used liberally; while spices, which were costly imports from the East, were used far more sparingly.

It was during the nineteenth century and with the Industrial Revolution that the mass-production of synthetic substitutes for herbs and flavourings began. Since then, so much has been done to food in the name of preserving, processing, making more 'attractive' and 'assuring a long shelf life', that some original flavours, colours and aromas have been lost. The rediscovery of the art of cooking with herbs has brought much pleasure and a reawakening of interest in growing them.

Facts and fables about herbs

Herbs are interesting and rewarding to grow. Each plant has its own characteristic flavour and scent. They may be used in cooking, in making fragrant and beneficial *tisanes* or teas, or gathered and dried for pot-pourri or sweet-smelling sachets. Every herb has its legend too, and it is almost worth growing them for this alone.

Angelica: Herbalists of old had faith in it as an antiseptic and country folk were firmly convinced that those who carry a piece of the root in their pockets are protected from witchcraft, the evil eye, and ill spirits. It has also been claimed that, if taken regularly in medicinal form (as an infusion, or fluid extract from the root) the herb will cause an aversion to alcohol.

Balm: Is known as balsam, lemon balm and Melissa. The Queen of Sheba is said to have taken seeds of balsam or balm as a present to King Solomon, and scented bushes from the seeds grew in Jericho. Many years later Cleopatra took cuttings of these plants to Mataria. Later still, during their flight to Egypt, Joseph, Mary, and Jesus took refuge in these fragrant balsam gardens. John Evelyn wrote, 'Balm is a sovereign remedy for the brain, strengthening the memory and powerfully chasing away melancholy.'

Basil: Though it is very pleasant to taste, useful in cooking, and has a peculiar sweet fragrance, for some unknown reason it has been connected with curses in all legends. The Romans were convinced of its 'contrariness', since they trod the ground underfoot with curses after they had planted the seed, calling on their Gods to make sure it did not flourish. In the Middle Ages opinion changed and there came the belief that basil would flourish only if planted and tended by a beautiful woman.

Borage: Known for increasing the refreshing quality of any liquid in which it is immersed. The bright blue flowers and silvery leaves are used today in Pimms No. 1 and claret cups. This beautiful plant also has the reputation for raising the spirits. The Greeks have a proverb, 'I, borage, bring always courage', and the Welsh gave it a name meaning the Herb of Gladness.

Bay: Native to Mediterranean areas, its leaves were once made into wreaths to crown the heroes of ancient Greece and Rome. Bay trees will grow in England, and can be cut back without any adverse effect. They are often seen growing at entrance doors in tubs. Culpeper wrote in the seventeenth century: 'Neither witch nor devil, thunder nor lightning, will hurt a man where a bay tree is.'

Dill: A great favourite of Scandinavia, Central Europe, Russia and America. Apart from its unusual flavour it has digestive and sedative qualities. Its name comes from the Norse word *dilla*, to lull, and its power is illustrated by its traditional use in babies' gripewater. It is possible that it quietens the baby by easing its digestion and thus makes it sleep. At one time dill seeds, called 'Meeting House' seeds, were eaten in church in the early morning to prevent people from feeling hungry.

Fennel: This is one of the earliest known herbs. It is mentioned in the early Anglo-Saxon herbals; it was regarded as one of nine sacred herbs, and its properties were said to have great physical benefits and to guard against unseen evil. In the Middle Ages keyholes were plugged with it to keep away ghosts. One of its ancient uses was for the restoration of eyesight; another use was as a decoction 'to make those more lean that are too fat'.

Marjoram: Has been a popular herb throughout its long history; mainly due to the fact that it has preserving and disinfectant qualities, which—before the days of refrigeration—made it invaluable in the kitchen. It was used medicinally for a number of complaints, from digestive disorders to curing toothache. It was also highly valued as a 'strewing' herb on the floors of houses.

The Mints: Besides being very strong and sweet, all the mint varieties have valuable properties. Culpeper describes a formidable number of diseases in which preparations of this herb were used medicinally. Mint has the reputation of repelling fleas, and it was used as a strewing herb in the Middle Ages.

Oregano: One of the marjorams, but its leaves are more pungent and hot, especially when grown in a warmer climate. The name Origanum comes from the Greek meaning 'joy of the mountains'.

Parsley: Cannot be surpassed for its versatility, it will go in every dish. It has been in demand from ancient times when it was considered a general panacea and all parts of the plant were used. One belief is that if the seeds are sown on Good Friday they will bring happiness and good fortune; another that if parsley is planted round the onion bed it will keep away the onion fly; and another that if parsley is thrown into a fish pond, it will cure sick fish.

Rosemary: Most of the legends wrapped around this aromatic shrub are mystical or sacred. The French believed the flowers rekindled lost energy, and they sometimes burnt branches of the bush for incense. Sprigs of rosemary to this day symbolise remembrance and friendship. There is a holy legend that during the flight to Egypt, the Virgin Mary threw her robe over a rosemary bush while she rested beside it. For ever afterwards the flowers which were previously white became blue.

Rue: Known as the 'herb of grace', it should be nearby, for 'where there's rosemary there's rue'. This was once a well-known ingredient for a tea in country districts and considered a remedy against dizziness and female disorders!

55

Sage: The custom of combining it with onions to stuff a rich meat, arose from the knowledge that sage aids digestion. There is an old Latin proverb, 'Why should a man die while a sage bush grows in his garden?' Other proverbs testify to the belief that sage ensures long life.

Tarragon: Belongs to same family as wormwood, southernwood, and mugwort, renowned for curing bee-stings and valued as a general tonic. Nearly every cottage garden had a bush of southernwood, also known as Lad's Love or Old Man. Bitter-sweet in scent and flavour, it repels moths. Tarragon is the most palatable and its uses in the kitchen are many, especially in French *haute cuisine*.

Thyme: Considered the enchanted herb, it was thought that wild thyme has always been a favourite with fairies. In Roman times it was a remedy for melancholy. Culpeper wrote that an infusion drunk at night was a certain cure for 'the nightmare'.

Growing herbs

There is no mystique about growing herbs, most of them thrive under fairly normal conditions, and many of them have pretty leaves and flowers.

The best position for the permanent ones is a border between path and boundary on the east or west side. A sage bush can be most attractive on the corner of a path, and rosemary can form part of a hedge—it will stand being cut back. Mint, parsley, thyme and chives, which are probably used most often should be planted where they can be easily gathered. A sunny pathway planting of herbs within easy reach of the kitchen is an ideal.

Although herbs may grow among all the other plants in the garden, it is more satisfactory to have them together—you are not then having to search when you want them, and you can see at a glance what is available, when you look for ingredients in a recipe.

Compact arrangements: If you want to grow herbs in one place in the garden it is a good idea to distinguish their position in some unusual way. I have seen a wheel-garden made by placing an old cartwheel on prepared ground, and planting the herbs between the spokes. However, cartwheels are not easy to come by these days, but if you can find one remember to graduate the size of the herbs as they radiate from the centre. The tall, bushy ones such as sage and rosemary can grow in the middle and the low border plants like chives, mint, parsley and thyme should be planted on the edges. Old ladders are easier to get, and give an interesting effect.

An old herb garden: If you have plenty of room in your garden, choose a sunny position and grow herbs in beds divided up by low-growing hedges, as in the Tudor 'knotted' or 'knot' garden. Clipped dwarf box hedges look neat, but herbs like lavender, savory and rosemary make good sweet-scented hedges.

The best time to start a herb garden is in the spring. Then, seeds which have been started in seed boxes after the frosts, can be planted out. On the whole they need a sunny aspect and a light soil. Only a few herbs such as chervil and bergamot prefer semi-shade.

Once the seedlings are planted out, they come on quickly if well cared for. Also, they respond to constant picking, become sturdier and more bushy. Pick parsley and chervil from the outside, to allow new leaves to grow from the middle, while basil needs to be picked from the top to prevent it flowering too soon.

Herb lawns

Some herbs can even be planted as lawns or along pathways because, like grass, they are hardy enough to be trodden upon. Most suitable for planting in this way are thyme, pennyroyal (a mint variety) and camomile. Pennyroyal is the most hardy. It spreads quickly and once it has formed a thick mat it discourages weeds. A delightful fresh peppermint scent comes up to meet you as it is trodden on. Camomile makes a good lawn. It needs regular mowing but will take as much traffic as ordinary grass. Thyme, however, is a little more delicate and needs a corner where it will not be trampled too often.

Growing herbs without a garden

If you live in a flat you can still grow a few herbs to pick and add fresh to some of your more adventurous dishes. You will need to get the right soil—a mixture of sand, leaf-mould and soil in equal parts—to put in your containers. Also, sunny window ledges to put them on. Remember, of course, to keep them watered, and every two weeks add a little liquid fertiliser to the watering can.

Even some of the taller varieties will grow in containers, because

with a confined root space they become usefully dwarfed. Herbs like basil, chives, chervil, marjoram, parsley and thyme are low growing and no problem. Herbs like mint with their spreading root system should be potted on their own, otherwise they will choke the others out. Some like angelica, lovage and one or two others grow too high to be considered. But rosemary and bay make attractive little indoor trees, will stand cutting back, and can be given fresh soil each year and be re-potted if necessary.

Window boxes make ideal containers for miniature herb gardens, but apart from these there are some attractive and useful containers on the market. It is worth searching out unusual ones to contain, for instance, a bay tree which can stand in a sitting room. Ordinary large flower pots are excellent on kitchen window ledges and they can be easily moved about, for the sun or for cleaning purposes. A trough of pottery, plastic (this can be painted), or metal, can have several herbs grouped together, and stand on a window-sill.

Patios, balconies and walls

If you have any little space out of doors such as a balcony or paved back-yard, you can always grow a few herbs. Strawberry pots look good, and a herb (small growing variety) can be planted in each of the pockets, while a taller and more decorative plant can grow in the top. Remember to put crocks in the bottom of pots to keep the soil well-drained. A sunny wall can have pots containing herbs hanging on it; a low cavity wall is also an excellent site.

58

Drying herbs

Herbs should be harvested just before the buds open into full flowers, this is when they have the most flavour and natural oils. Pick them in dry weather, after the dew has left them and before the sun has started to draw out the oils. Hang them up to dry in bundles, stalks up and heads down, in an airy passageway or attic, or lay them out on paper in a dark cupboard. Oven-drying is not recommended unless the weather is wet, since a lot of flavour is lost this way. Drying time takes from twelve days to three weeks depending on the moisture in the air. When dry, strip the leaves from the stalks and pour them into clean, dry, airtight jars which should be clearly labelled.

A much smaller quantity of dried herbs is needed for flavouring than of those picked straight from the garden. As a general rule, if fresh herbs are called for in a recipe and you do not have them, use one-third of the amount of dried herbs.

Herb Flavouring Table

Bread, Cakes and Pastries: caraway, coriander, anise, angelica
Cheese—Hot Dishes: basil, marjoram, thyme, tarragon
Cream or Cottage Cheese: chives, mint, dill, sage, basil, caraway
Confectionary: mint, caraway, coriander, borage flowers, angelica
Egg Dishes: chives, tarragon, basil, marjoram, chervil, thyme
Desserts: mint, marjoram, caraway, anise
Fish: fennel, sage, thyme, basil, chives, chervil, parsley
Fruit Cup and Cold Beverages: mint, borage, balm, rosemary
Garnishes: parsley, thyme, rosemary, marjoram, balm, basil, chervil, savory
Jams and Jellies: mint, rosemary, balm
Meats: *Beef*—basil, marjoram, savory, thyme, rosemary
      Pork—sage, basil, rosemary, marjoram, chives
      Lamb—marjoram, savory, rosemary, dill, coriander
      Veal—rosemary, savory, thyme, sage
Pickles and Condiments: dill, tarragon, borage, sage, rosemary
Poultry: savory, tarragon, thyme, marjoram, sage
Salads: mint, chives, dill, basil, borage, fennel, tarragon, chervil, savory, thyme, balm, parsley

Sauces: *Meat and poultry*—dill, mint, tarragon, thyme, chervil, marjoram

Fish and shellfish —fennel, parsley, chervil, dill, thyme, mint, tarragon

Soups and stews —basil, marjoram, savory, parsley, thyme, mint, tarragon, chives, chervil

Teas: mint, sage, anise, balm, marjoram, thyme, camomile

Vegetables: *Beets*—basil, savory, fennel, caraway, coriander

Broad beans—parsley, fennel

Cabbage—mint, caraway, fennel, dill

Carrots—savory, mint, basil, parsley, thyme

Cucumber—dill, parsley, mint

Onions—tarragon, thyme

Peas—mint, savory, basil, rosemary

Potatoes—mint, parsley, basil, chives, fennel, caraway

Spinach—marjoram, mint

Tomatoes—basil, marjoram, sage

Turnips—chives, celery seed, fennel

Cooking facts

A half teaspoon of dried herbs is equivalent to two scant teaspoons fresh herbs. To bring out the aromatic oils in the leaves, buds and seeds, crush or chop fresh herbs before using; soak dried herbs in oil, wine or stock, then crush. Fine chopped herbs are called *fines herbes*. A faggot of herbs is a bunch tied together. Quantities given here are for fresh herbs, unless otherwise stated.

A *bouquet garni*, frequently mentioned in French cooking, is a mixture of aromatic herbs, usually parsley, thyme, bay leaves, tied in muslin and added to the cooking pot. There is no set rule and the mixture can vary according to individual preference.

Herbs to grow for cooking

balm	—*annual*	chervil	—*biennial*	parsley	—*biennial*
basil	—*annual*	chives	—*annual*	rosemary	—*perennial*
bay tree	—*perennial*	dill	—*annual*	sage	—*perennial*
bergamot	—*perennial*	fennel	—*annual*	savory	—*perennial*
borage	—*annual*	marjoram	—*perennial*	tarragon	—*perennial*
caraway	—*biennial*	mint	—*perennial*	thyme	—*perennial*
		oregano	—*perennial*		

Recipes

Soups

Cucumber and Mint Soup: Put 2 medium cucumbers, peeled and chopped, 2 cartons natural yogurt and 4–5 sprigs of fresh mint in a liquidiser and blend until smooth. Add salt and pepper to taste. Serve chilled and sprinkled with freshly chopped mint.

Spinach Soup with Egg

1 PINT COOKED SPINACH, SIEVED	GOOD PINCH NUTMEG
2 PINTS BEEF STOCK	1 EGG PER PERSON
SALT AND PEPPER	CREAM
	CHERVIL

Pour the sieved spinach into the beef stock. Heat, adding salt and pepper to taste and nutmeg. Meanwhile, boil the eggs for 4 minutes and shell them. Serve the hot soup with a whole egg, 1 tablespoon cream, and a generous sprinkling of chopped chervil in each plate.

Hot Cucumber Soup

4 OZ. SLICED LEEKS	$1\frac{1}{2}$ TEASPOONS SALT
1 LB. CHOPPED UNPEELED CUCUMBERS	$\frac{1}{2}$ TEASPOON POWDERED MUSTARD
8 OZ. FINELY CHOPPED RAW POTATOES	1 TABLESPOON CHOPPED SAVORY
4 TABLESPOONS CHOPPED PARSLEY	$\frac{1}{4}$ TEASPOON WHITE PEPPER
$1\frac{1}{2}$ PINTS CHICKEN STOCK	$\frac{1}{4}$ PINT DOUBLE CREAM

Wash the leeks well and slice them. Place in a saucepan with the cucumber, potatoes, parsley, stock, salt, mustard and savory. Cook until vegetables are tender. Strain through a sieve or liquidise. Heat. Just before serving add white pepper and stir well. Add a swirl of cream to each plate of soup.

Carrot and Orange Soup

I LB. CARROTS	I SPRIG LEMON THYME
I LARGE ONION	SALT AND PEPPER TO TASTE
I LARGE POTATO	I TEASPOON CORNFLOUR
I LARGE ORANGE	$\frac{1}{4}$ PINT MILK
I OZ. BUTTER	I TABLESPOON CHOPPED
2 CHICKEN STOCK CUBES	CHIVES

Peel and grate carrots, onion and potato. Grate zest from orange and squeeze the juice. Melt the butter in a strong saucepan, and sweat the grated vegetables in this until soft and turning golden. Add orange juice, stock cubes dissolved in $1\frac{1}{2}$ pints boiling water, and the lemon thyme. Add salt and pepper. Cover and simmer for 25 minutes. Mix cornflour to a smooth paste with a little milk. Add rest of milk to soup. Taste and adjust seasoning and thicken with the cornflour mixture. Simmer, uncovered, for a further 3 minutes. Serve sprinkled with chopped chives.

Cold Vegetable Cream Soup

I LARGE ONION	I PINT CHICKEN STOCK
I LARGE CARROT	SALT AND PEPPER TO TASTE
I LARGE POTATO	I EGG YOLK
2 LEEKS	$\frac{1}{4}$ PINT SINGLE CREAM
I OZ. BUTTER	
$1\frac{1}{2}$ TABLESPOONS FRESH MIXED	
CHOPPED HERBS (PARSLEY,	
TARRAGON, MARJORAM)	

Peel and grate the onion, carrot and potato. Clean and cut the leeks in fine rings. Melt the butter, add the herbs, then the vegetables. Stir and sweat in the butter until soft. Pour in the stock, add seasoning to taste, and cook, covered, for about 10 minutes. Beat in the egg yolk off the heat. Sieve or liquidise the mixture. Chill thoroughly. Stir in a little single cream before serving. Less refreshing than cold cucumber or tomato soups, perhaps, but it is surprising how delicious this type of soup tastes cold.

Scallops with Dill

I LB. SCALLOPS
2 TABLESPOONS FLOUR
I EGG
BREADCRUMBS FOR FRYING
3 OZ. BUTTER OR MARGARINE

SCANT ½ PINT STOCK OR MILK
I TABLESPOON SHERRY
I TABLESPOON FINELY
   CHOPPED DILL

Roll the scallops in just under half the flour. Then coat in the beaten egg and the breadcrumbs. Fry in the melted butter for a few minutes on either side. Remove scallops to a dish and keep hot. Stir the rest of the flour into the hot fat and blend well. Pour in the stock or milk and the sherry and stir until thick. Add the dill, pour the sauce over the scallops. Serve at once.

Halibut Pie

2 LB. HALIBUT
I SMALL ONION, FINELY
   CHOPPED
BASIL, CHIVES AND PARSLEY
2 OZ. BUTTER

½ OZ. FLOUR
2 HARD-BOILED EGGS
SALT AND PEPPER
6 OZ. FLAKY PASTRY
I EGG YOLK

Parboil the halibut with the onion in about ½ pint water. Remove flesh from the bones and put in a greased pie-dish with the onion.

Sprinkle with finely chopped basil, chives and parsley. If preferred, fennel can be substituted for these herbs. Melt 1½ oz. butter in a pan and cook flour in this for 2–3 minutes, pour in the fish liquor and stir until smooth. Pour this sauce over the fish. Slice the hard-boiled eggs and place them on top, dotted with the rest of the butter and sprinkle with salt and pepper to taste. Cover with flaky pastry. Brush this with beaten egg yolk. Bake in a hot oven for 30 minutes.

Fish in Walnut Sauce

1½ LB. COOKED FLAKED FISH
1 PINT WHITE SAUCE
SALT, PEPPER, GRATED NUTMEG
  TO SEASON

1 TABLESPOON CHOPPED CHIVES
2 TEASPOONS CHOPPED PARSLEY
2 TEASPOONS CHOPPED
  WALNUTS

Stir the fish (haddock, halibut or cod or a mixture) into the white sauce. Season with salt, pepper and a little nutmeg. Put into an ovenproof dish and sprinkle with the herbs and walnuts. Place in a moderate oven for about 20 minutes. Serve with slices of lemon. The mixture can be baked in scallop shells, topped with a ring of mashed potato, for special occasions.

Fish with Dill and Parsley Sauce

1 LB. FRESH HADDOCK FILLET
1 LB. COD FILLET
SALT
1 SMALL ONION
1 CELERY STALK, CHOPPED
1 BAY LEAF
FEW STALKS PARSLEY

1 OZ. BUTTER
1 OZ. FLOUR
1 CUBE SUGAR
1 TEASPOON DRIED DILL
1 TABLESPOON CHOPPED PARSLEY
SALT AND PEPPER
1 EGG YOLK

Sprinkle salt on fish and leave for 1 hour. Simmer onion, celery, bay leaf, and parsley stalks in salted water for 20 minutes. Put fish into boiling stock, bring back to boil, reduce heat and simmer, covered, for 10 minutes. Remove from heat and add 2 tablespoons cold water. Take out fish and arrange on serving dish, keep warm. Melt the butter, stir in the flour, add ½ pint strained fish stock, sugar and dill. Cook gently for 5 minutes, stirring, then add the chopped parsley. Remove from heat, add salt and pepper to taste, beat in the egg yolk. Pour sauce over the fish.

EGGS AND CHEESE

Soufflé Omelette aux Fines Herbes

3 EGGS	SALT AND PEPPER
I OZ. BUTTER	I–2 TEASPOONS CHOPPED
2 TABLESPOONS WARM WATER	CHIVES OR MIXED HERBS

Separate the whites from yolks of eggs. Melt the butter in the pan. Beat the yolks and add the warm water and seasoning to taste. Beat egg whites until stiff, then fold into the yolks. Pour into the hot, well-distributed butter in the pan. Turn heat low underneath. When the omelette has risen and is golden underneath, sprinkle the herbs on top and put under a low grill for a few minutes to finish cooking. Fold over, lift from pan and serve immediately.

Variation: Sprinkle a tablespoon of grated cheese and a teaspoon of chopped sage on the omelette before grilling.

Breakfast Eggs: Poaching cups with screw tops are best for these, but an ordinary egg poaching unit can be used. Grease the cup or container and put in a pinch of a preferred dried herb or a mixture. If using fresh herbs, put about I teaspoon. Break the egg and pour it in and mix the white in with the herbs, carefully from the bottom, to distribute herbs more evenly. Seal poaching cups and cook in hot water, or poach in the usual way.

Stuffed Eggs aux Fines Herbes: Cut 4 hard-boiled eggs in half lengthwise. Remove yolks, mash and mix with I teaspoon prepared mustard, I teaspoon mayonnaise, salt and pepper to taste, I tablespoon mixed herbs (see omelette). Fill the whites, heaping full, with the mixture and sprinkle with chopped parsley and paprika.

Scrambled Eggs: Various herb combinations make scrambled eggs interesting and tasty, e.g. chopped mint and chives or parsley, the amount of chives varying to suit individual taste. Lemon thyme can be used alone, or a blend of chopped ham with a little sage and chopped chives. Used cold, these scrambled egg blends make excellent sandwich fillings.

C

Welsh Rarebit with Sage

¼ PINT BEER
8 OZ. GRATED CHEESE (MATURE CHEDDAR)
2 TEASPOONS SAGE LEAVES

SALT AND PEPPER
½ TEASPOON MUSTARD
TOAST

Warm the beer and gradually add the cheese, finely chopped sage, salt and pepper to taste, and mustard. Stir well until the cheese has melted. Use to cover slices of buttered toast. Place under a hot grill for a few minutes to brown. Serve at once.

Herbed Cheese Pot

I LB. GRATED CHEDDAR CHEESE
3 OZ. CREAM CHEESE
4 TABLESPOONS OLIVE OIL
I TEASPOON MUSTARD POWDER

½ TEASPOON MARJORAM
½ TEASPOON TARRAGON
4 TABLESPOONS SHERRY

Combine the cheeses and mix in the oil until smooth. Blend in the mustard and herbs and sherry. Put into a jar and store in refrigerator to use as needed. Serve on toast or crisp biscuits. (It will keep for 2 weeks.)

Minted Cheese Tart

6 OZ. SHORTCRUST PASTRY
8 OZ. CREAM CHEESE
2–3 TABLESPOONS TOP OF MILK
I THINLY SLICED UNPEELED CUCUMBER

6 EGGS
SALT AND PEPPER
3 TABLESPOONS FINELY CHOPPED MINT

Line a pie dish with a thin pastry layer. Mash the cream cheese with milk and spread on top. Cover cheese with cucumber. Break the eggs on to this, season well and strew the top with mint. Bake for about 30 minutes in a moderate oven until pastry is golden and eggs set.

Mint and Marshmallow Custard: Beat together with a fork, in an ovenproof dish, 3 eggs and 1 tablespoon sugar. Gradually mix in 1 pint milk. Sprinkle with 2 tablespoons very finely chopped mint (or two teaspoons dried mint) and float about 24 marshmallows on top. Stand the dish in a shallow container of hot water, and bake in a moderate oven until custard is set. Can be eaten hot or cold; the marshmallows become caramelised, and the mint counteracts the sweetness.

Herb Pancakes: For savoury pancakes a variety of chopped herbs can be blended into the mixture. Dried sage and grated onion for instance, with chopped ham rolled inside before serving. Oregano in the mixture is good with minced or chopped beef folded inside the cooked pancake. Herb pancakes also taste good eaten cold.

MEAT, POULTRY AND GAME

Steak Flambé with Marjoram

4 PIECES FILLET STEAK
1½ OZ. BUTTER
4–6 TABLESPOONS BRANDY

SALT AND PEPPER
2 TABLESPOONS FINELY
CHOPPED MARJORAM

Put the steaks in a heavy frying pan with the melted butter. Brown them well on each side. Cook for 2–4 minutes on each side, according to whether preferred rare or well done. Pour the brandy over them and set it alight. When the flames have died down put the steaks on a hot dish. Pour liquor from the pan over them, sprinkle with salt and freshly ground pepper. Top with the marjoram.

Herbed Meat Balls

1 LB. BRAISING STEAK, MINCED
1½ TEASPOONS SALT
½ TEASPOON CHOPPED THYME
1 TABLESPOON CHOPPED
  PARSLEY
½ GARLIC CLOVE, CRUSHED
PINCH CAYENNE PEPPER
1 OZ. FINE, DRY BREADCRUMBS

1 EGG
2 TABLESPOONS COOKING OIL
¼ PINT BEEF STOCK
2 TABLESPOONS TOMATO
  PURÉE
1 TABLESPOON MINCED ONION
6 TABLESPOONS SOUR CREAM

Mix the beef with one teaspoon of salt, the herbs, garlic, cayenne, breadcrumbs and egg to bind. Form into balls. Brown in the oil. Add the stock and tomato purée, the onion and remaining ½ teaspoon salt. Bring to the boil and simmer for 5 minutes. Stir in cream. Heat only until cream is hot.

Boiled Silverside with Herb Dumplings

2–3 LB. SALTED SILVERSIDE OF
  BEEF
BOUQUET GARNI
4 SMALL ONIONS

2 STICKS CELERY
4 CARROTS
2 YOUNG TURNIPS

Soak the beef for several hours, changing the water once or twice to get rid of excess salt. Put into a large saucepan, cover with water, add the bouquet garni and bring slowly to the boil. Remove scum and simmer, covered, for 1½ hours. Add the sliced vegetables (keep onions whole), and cook slowly for another 45 minutes. 20 minutes before serving add small dumplings made with:

4 OZ. SELF-RAISING FLOUR
2 OZ. SHREDDED SUET
SALT AND PEPPER TO TASTE
COLD WATER

½ SMALL ONION, FINELY
  GRATED
½ TEASPOON MIXED DRIED
  HERBS

Mix all these ingredients together with enough cold water to make a sticky dough. Divide into 12–16 portions, roll into small balls, with floured hands, simmer in the broth for 20 minutes.

Beef Casserole with Pickled Walnuts

I LB. STEWING STEAK
2 TABLESPOONS FLOUR
2 BAY LEAVES
I ONION, FINELY SLICED

2 TOMATOES, SLICED
4 PICKLED WALNUTS, HALVED
SALT, PEPPER AND SUGAR
⅓ PINT RED WINE OR STOCK

Cut the steak into cubes and roll well in the flour. Put layers of the steak, bay leaves, onion, tomatoes, pickled walnuts in a casserole, adding salt and pepper to taste and a small sprinkling of sugar. Add any left-over flour and pour over the wine or stock. Cook covered in a slow oven for 2 hours.

Sweetbreads with Basil

8 OZ. BACON
2 OZ. BUTTER OR MARGARINE
I LB. LAMB'S SWEETBREADS
2 TABLESPOONS SEASONED FLOUR

½ PINT STOCK
2 TABLESPOONS CHOPPED
  BASIL

Grill the bacon, or fry in its own fat, and put on a dish in a warm place. Melt the butter, and gently cook the sweetbreads which have been cut up and rolled in the flour. Add stock and basil and cook for further 5 minutes. Arrange the fry with the bacon on the dish, and pour the gravy over.

Note: Lamb's sweetbreads are not always easy to obtain, but calves' sweetbreads can be used instead.

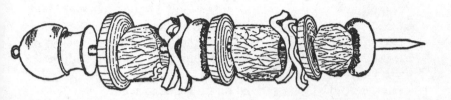

Skewered Lamb with Rosemary

2½–3 LB. LEG OF LAMB
1 TEASPOON SALT
1 TEASPOON GARLIC SALT
2 TEASPOONS CRUMBLED
  ROSEMARY LEAVES
½ TEASPOON GROUND BLACK
  PEPPER
2 TABLESPOONS PREPARED
  MUSTARD

2 TABLESPOONS CIDER
  VINEGAR
4 TABLESPOONS OLIVE OIL
16 SMALL ONION SLICES
16 SQUARES OF GREEN PEPPER
16 WHOLE, FRESH BUTTON
  MUSHROOMS

Trim away the excess fat from the meat and cut the lean portion into 1½-inch cubes. Combine the salts, rosemary, pepper, mustard, vinegar and oil together and pour over the meat. Leave meat marinating in this mixture in refrigerator overnight or for 5–6 hours, turning meat in the marinade several times. String the lamb on eight skewers, alternating with onion slices, bits of green pepper and mushrooms. Cook under a low grill, turning and basting with the marinade until thoroughly cooked all round.

Variation: The ingredients used to thread on the skewers can be varied by using very small, slightly under-ripe tomatoes instead of the mushrooms. This is a useful way to use up some of the last tomatoes to ripen on your plants.

69

Smith's Hot-pot

8 OZ. POTATOES	1 TEASPOON CHOPPED
2 LB. LEAN PORK	MARJORAM
1 ONION	2 TEASPOONS CHOPPED
1 APPLE	PARSLEY
2 STICKS CELERY	PEPPER AND SALT
1 TEASPOON CHOPPED SAGE	STOCK OR WATER TO COVER

Peel the potatoes and slice fairly thickly. Place in the bottom of a casserole. Cut the meat into cubes, and arrange in layers with sliced onion, apple, celery, sprinkling the herbs and seasoning between the layers. Just cover with stock or water. Place lid on casserole and cook for 2 hours in a slow oven. The old smithy fire always had an iron pot of stew, such as this one, keeping hot nearby until the blacksmith could find time to eat it.

Meat 'Ducks'

8 OZ. SAUSAGE MEAT	PEPPER, SALT AND DRY
3 PARBOILED ONIONS, MINCED	MUSTARD TO TASTE
3 TABLESPOONS SOFT	2 TABLESPOONS FLOUR
BREADCRUMBS	1 OZ. LARD OR DRIPPING
1 TEASPOON CHOPPED SAGE	1 APPLE, PEELED AND CORED

Mix sausage meat, onions, breadcrumbs, sage and seasonings to taste. Form into round cakes, coat in flour, fry in hot fat until brown. Slice apple into rings and fry until golden and tender. Serve the 'ducks' with apple rings on top, with vegetables or on toast.

Scrumpy Sausages

8 SAUSAGES	2 CLOVES GARLIC
2 TABLESPOONS FLOUR	1 TEASPOON CHOPPED SAGE
1 OZ. LARD	2 TEASPOONS PARSLEY
2 APPLES, CORED BUT UNPEELED	SALT AND PEPPER
4 SHALLOTS OR SMALL ONIONS	$\frac{1}{2}$ PINT CIDER

Skin sausages and roll in flour. Fry lightly all over in hot lard. Put them into a casserole with layers of sliced apple, finely chopped shallots, finely chopped garlic, the herbs and salt and pepper to taste. Add the cider. Cover and cook for 1 hour in a moderate oven.

Note: The name of the recipe refers to the drink scrumpy, which is a rough kind of cider.

Pork Chop Pockets

4 THICK PORK CHOPS	½ TEASPOON SALT
2 OZ. SOFT BREADCRUMBS	PEPPER TO TASTE
1 TABLESPOON GRATED ONION	*Garnish :*
1 APPLE, GRATED	1 RED-SKINNED APPLE
1 OZ. BUTTER, MELTED	1 TABLESPOON HONEY
1 TABLESPOON CHOPPED PARSLEY	FRESHLY GRATED NUTMEG
1 TEASPOON CHOPPED SAGE	

Make a pocket in each chop by slitting meat to the bone. Mix breadcrumbs, grated onion, apple, butter, herbs and seasoning. Stuff the pockets in the chops with this mixture; secure the openings with wooden picks. Bake in a shallow casserole in a moderate oven until well browned, about 20 minutes. Core the remaining apple and cut into 4 thick slices and arrange one slice on each chop. Brush with honey and sprinkle with nutmeg. Add 3 tablespoons hot water. Cover and bake until chops are tender and apple glazed, 40–50 minutes.

Herb Liver Grill

2 RASHERS STREAKY BACON	½ TEASPOON CHOPPED MARJORAM
1 LB. 8 OZ. LAMB'S LIVER	½ TEASPOON CHOPPED THYME
1 OZ. MELTED BUTTER	SALT TO TASTE
1 TABLESPOON LEMON JUICE	⅛ TEASPOON BLACK PEPPER

Remove rind from bacon and chop finely. Trim liver and place on a greased grill rack. Mix together the other ingredients. Spread half over the liver and place under grill. Grill for about 8 minutes until browned. Turn liver and spread the rest of seasoned butter. Grill for 6 minutes, or until done. Serve with drippings from pan poured over the liver.

Kidney Casserole

2 TEASPOONS SALT	1 TEASPOON SUGAR
2 LB. VEAL OR LAMB'S KIDNEY	1 TEASPOON CHOPPED BASIL
1½ OZ. BUTTER OR MARGARINE	1 TEASPOON CHOPPED OREGANO
8 OZ. RIPE TOMATOES	¼ TEASPOON BLACK PEPPER
4 CELERY STALKS, CHOPPED	4 OZ. BUTTON MUSHROOMS
1 LARGE ONION, CHOPPED	

Rub 1 teaspoon of salt over the kidneys and let them stand 2 hours to remove some of the strong flavour. Rinse in cold water. Remove membrane and white tubes and cut into ¼-inch thick slices. Sauté for 5 minutes in the fat, then add tomatoes, celery, onion and sugar. Cover and simmer for 30 minutes. Add herbs, pepper, mushrooms and remaining salt. Cook for another 10 minutes.

Tripe in Tomato Sauce

1½ LB. TRIPE	1 TEASPOON DRIED OREGANO
2 OZ. FLOUR	2 TEASPOONS CHOPPED BASIL
2 OZ. BUTTER	1 PINT STOCK OR WATER
3 LARGE ONIONS	SALT AND CAYENNE PEPPER
1 CLOVE GARLIC	TO TASTE
4 TABLESPOONS TOMATO PURÉE	

Make sure the butcher has blanched the tripe. Cut the tripe into slices, and dredge well with half the flour. Melt the butter; cook the tripe gently in it for about 10 minutes. Add the sliced onions and the crushed clove of garlic. Thicken with the rest of the flour and tomato purée smoothing out lumps. Add oregano and basil. Gradually add stock, stirring. Season with salt and cayenne. Cook in covered casserole in a very slow oven for 2½–3 hours.

Chicken with Tarragon

1 ROASTING CHICKEN (ABOUT 3 LB.)	SALT AND PEPPER
	1 TEASPOON FLOUR
1 TABLESPOON CHOPPED TARRAGON	¼ PINT CREAM
	2 TABLESPOONS CHOPPED
4 OZ. BUTTER	TARRAGON

Wipe chicken. Work the tablespoon of tarragon into 2 oz. butter, season with salt and pepper and put inside the bird. Put the rest of the butter in a heavy casserole with lid and put chicken in this, lying on its side in the butter, turn it over after 45 minutes, baste every now and again with the butter. Cook until tender, about 1½ hours in a moderate oven. Remove to a serving dish and stir the flour into the juices in the casserole. When this is smooth, add the cream and tarragon. Bring just to the boil and when it has thickened pour it over the chicken.

Chicken Livers in Wine

1 LB. 8 OZ. CHICKEN LIVERS
4 OZ. BUTTER
2 CLOVES GARLIC, FINELY
  CHOPPED
2 TEASPOONS CHOPPED
  TARRAGON

2 TEASPOONS CHOPPED
  MARJORAM
1 TABLESPOON FLOUR
SALT AND PEPPER
½ PINT RED OR WHITE WINE

Wash chicken livers, cut into neat pieces, and simmer gently in the melted butter with the garlic until cooked, but still slightly pink inside. Add tarragon, marjoram, flour and seasoning to taste. Cook, turning the livers, until flour browns. Gradually add the wine, stirring until the gravy is smooth and thickened. Serve with boiled rice. A rich stock can be used instead of wine if preferred.

Harvest Rabbit

2 SMALL RABBITS
DRIPPING TO FRY
6 PRUNES, WELL SOAKED
2 BUNCHES FRESH HERBS
SEASONED FLOUR
4 ONIONS, SLICED
2 SLICES FAT BACON
STOCK
Forcemeat Balls:
4 OZ. CHOPPED BACON

1 TABLESPOON CHOPPED
  CHIVES
2 TEASPOONS CHOPPED
  MARJORAM
1 TABLESPOON CHOPPED
  PARSLEY
SALT AND PEPPER
6 OZ. SOFT BREADCRUMBS
1 EGG

Wash the skinned rabbits well and leave in salt water for 15 minutes. Dry and fry whole in heated dripping until a pale golden all over. Drain, and stuff under the ribs of each rabbit 3 prunes and a bunch of fresh herbs. Coat thickly with well-seasoned flour. Cover the bottom of a large, deep baking dish with the sliced onions, lay the floured rabbits on them, with a slice of fat bacon over each, and just cover with stock. Bake in a slow oven for 2 hours. Serve on a hot dish garnished with the onions and forcemeat balls, made of the ingredients above, bound with the egg and fried a deep brown in very hot fat.

Note: Traditionally the young rabbits caught in the stubble at harvest time are used for this dish.

Fruited Chicken Pie

1 BOILING FOWL (ABOUT 4 LB.)
1 CARROT
1 ONION
1 BAY LEAF
SALT AND PEPPER
8 OZ. HAM, IN THICK SLICES
3 OZ. DRIED APRICOTS
1 SMALL ONION, FINELY
    CHOPPED
3 TEASPOONS THYME OR
    CHERVIL, CHOPPED
10 OZ. SHORT OR FLAKY PASTRY
1 BEATEN EGG

Simmer the chicken with the chopped carrot and onion, and bay leaf, in sufficient water to just cover, seasoned with a little salt and pepper. After about 1 hour (when flesh is fairly tender but still firm), remove chicken from saucepan and slice off the meat. Put a layer at the bottom of a pie dish, then a layer of roughly chopped ham and apricots. Sprinkle lightly with finely chopped onion and thyme or chervil. Fill the dish with layers in that order. Pour over sufficient chicken stock to moisten, and adjust seasoning to taste. Put on pastry lid, making a small hole in top for steam to escape. Glaze with beaten egg. Cook for 1 hour in a moderately hot oven (covering with greaseproof paper if the pastry becomes too brown). The quantity given will make one very large pie or two small ones.

Gamekeeper's Pie: A similar pie was often made in the shires, with old partridges, or an old pheasant. In this case, the apricots were replaced by dried apple rings. The beauty of this type of pie is that it is equally good hot or cold, makes a hearty meal at a moment's notice without the trouble of reheating, or can stand being reheated very well indeed. The gamekeeper who gave me this recipe baked it himself and ate it cold for breakfast, hot for mid-day dinner and cold for supper until it was finished.

Suffolk Jugged Hare

1 HARE	A STRIP OF LEMON PEEL
2 TABLESPOONS FLOUR	1½ OZ. BUTTER
A BUNCH OF FRESH HERBS	1 TABLESPOON FLOUR
2 ONIONS (EACH STUCK WITH 3 CLOVES)	2 TABLESPOONS TOMATO KETCHUP
6 WHOLE ALLSPICE	LITTLE PORT WINE (OPTIONAL)
½ TEASPOON BLACK PEPPER	

Wash hare and cut into small joints. Flour each piece thoroughly. Put into saucepan with herbs, onions, allspice, pepper and lemon peel. Cover with hot water and let it simmer until tender. Take out hare, heat butter and cook flour in it for 1 minute, stirring, then gradually add the stock from saucepan. Add ketchup and port wine and allow to boil for 10 minutes, then strain through a sieve over the hare and serve very hot with red-currant jelly.

VEGETABLES

Parsley Ice

JUICE 1 LEMON	½ PINT WATER
FINELY GRATED ZEST 1 LEMON	1 TABLESPOON DRY SHERRY
4 OZ. SUGAR	GREEN FOOD COLOURING
2 TABLESPOONS FINELY CHOPPED PARSLEY	1 EGG WHITE, STIFFLY BEATEN

Put juice and lemon zest in a saucepan with sugar and water. Bring to the boil and stir in parsley. Simmer for 5 minutes. Cool, add the sherry and few drops of green colouring. Put in an ice tray and freeze. When forming crystals take out and mix into the beaten egg white. Return to refrigerator to harden. It looks tempting turned out on to a dish, and can be served as an unusual accompaniment to a meat course.

Creamed Mushrooms

8 OZ. MUSHROOMS	2 TABLESPOONS FLOUR
1 TABLESPOON MIXED MARJORAM,	½ TEASPOON SALT
CHERVIL, BASIL	4 TABLESPOONS CREAM
2 THICK SLICES LEMON	4 SLICES TOAST
2 TABLESPOONS BUTTER	

Wipe the mushrooms clean. Put into a saucepan with the herbs, in a muslin bag, and the lemon and enough water to cover them. Cook until the mushrooms are tender and the water is reduced to about ¼ pint. Remove herbs and lemon, strain and save liquid. Heat the butter and blend in the flour and salt. Add the mushroom stock and the cream gradually, stirring all the time, to make a medium thick sauce. Add more cream or milk if necessary. Stir in mushrooms, simmer gently for another 5 minutes and serve on toast as a supper dish or savoury.

Minted Bananas: Fry sliced bananas lightly in butter with plenty of chopped-up mint to accompany crumbed cutlets.

SAUCES AND DRESSINGS

Boiled Mustard and Dill Sauce: Stir 2 teaspoons mustard powder into a paste with 1 teaspoon anchovy essence and 2 teaspoons of vinegar. Melt 1 oz. butter, stir in 1 oz. flour, add just under ½ pint milk, bring to the boil. Stir in the mustard mixture, chopped dill, and salt to taste. Bring to the boil and simmer for another 5 minutes.

Fennel Cream Sauce: Whip ¼ pint double cream until thick but not fluffy. Stir in a teaspoon honey, 1 tablespoon lemon juice, blending well. Add 2 tablespoons finely chopped fennel and season to taste. Serve with fish.

Sauce Tartare: Put an egg yolk in a basin with ½ teaspoon dry mustard, ¼ teaspoon each salt and pepper. Gradually drop 4 oz. olive oil on to this, stirring well all the time until mixture is smooth and thick. Beat in 1 tablespoon tarragon vinegar carefully and add 2 teaspoons chopped olives, 1 teaspoon chopped capers, 2 teaspoons chopped tarragon. Serve with fish.

Balm Dressing for Orange Salad: Peel 4 large oranges, cut into slices and lay in a dish with some thinly sliced deseeded green peppers. Make a dressing with 1 tablespoon herb vinegar, to 3 tablespoons oil, and stir in 1 tablespoon finely chopped balm. Pour over the oranges and allow to marinate for a few hours before serving. Excellent with roast duck.

Mint and Cheese Dressing: Take 1 tablespoon mint leaves, chopped very finely, pound a small clove of garlic and mix thoroughly with 6–8 oz. cream cheese. Bake some potatoes, scrubbed and rubbed with oil, in their jackets—this takes $1-1\frac{1}{2}$ hours in a moderately hot oven. When cooked slit potatoes making a cross on top and squeeze them open. Serve with the cheese mixture pushed inside the cavity.

DRINKS

Balm and Orange Frosted: Mix a pint of orange juice with $\frac{1}{2}$ pint lemon juice, 1 pint water, 4 oz. sugar. Add a bunch of balm leaves and chill overnight. Strain and add 2 bottles ginger ale just before serving and pour into glasses over cubes of ice. Float a balm leaf on the top of each drink.

Pineapple Cocktail: Peel pineapple and slice downwards. Cut into cubes and strain the juice into a saucepan with 2 tablespoons finely chopped mint and 8 oz. sugar. Bring to boil and simmer for 2 minutes. Pour back on to pineapple. Chill and serve as an appetiser in individual dishes garnished with a sprig of mint and a cherry. The core and peel of pineapple can be simmered with sugar and water for about 45 minutes, the liquid strained off and chilled for drinks.

Mint in Tea: Mint leaves mixed in packaged tea can impart a delicious flavour.

BISCUITS AND BREADS

Herb Biscuits: Biscuits to eat plain or buttered with cheese can be given an interesting flavour by sprinkling herbs into a short-crust pastry mixture, using yolk of 1 egg and milk to mix.

Herbs to use: basil with lovage, tarragon with chives, mixed herbs including lemon thyme and oregano, and rosemary. Allow an average of 2 tablespoons fresh mixed herbs to 1 lb. flour.

Herb Bread

2 TEASPOONS DRIED YEAST	2 TABLESPOONS CHOPPED
¼ PINT WARM MILK	FRESH HERBS
¼ PINT WARM WATER	2 TEASPOONS MIXED DRIED
2 TEASPOONS CASTER SUGAR	HERBS
1 OZ. BUTTER, MELTED	*Topping :*
2 TEASPOONS SALT	½ OZ. MELTED BUTTER
1 LB. PLAIN FLOUR	½ TEASPOON MIXED DRIED
	HERBS

Soak the yeast in the warm milk and water with 2 teaspoons sugar —when it rises and bubbles it is ready for use. Mix with the butter, salt and 8 oz. flour. Mix well. Cover and allow to rise in a warm place, about 1 hour. Add herbs to the mixture. Stir in rest of flour to make a stiff dough. Knead on a floured board until satiny and elastic. Place in a greased bowl, cover and leave in a warm place until it doubles its bulk. Punch dough down and leave it for 10 minutes. Shape 1 lb. of dough into a loaf and put into a greased loaf tin. Use remaining dough for a round loaf or 6 rolls. Brush tops with melted butter and sprinkling of dried herbs. Leave to rise till double in size. Bake in preheated oven, moderately hot, for 50 minutes or until cooked.

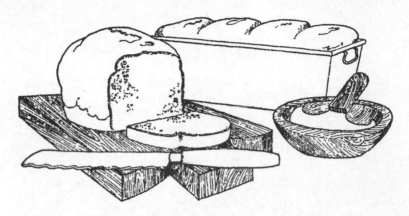

Herbed Loaf: This method of serving a French loaf, or round cob loaf, is especially suitable when the bread is slightly stale and requires crisping up. It is delicious for Sunday parties, or at any time when freshly baked bread is not available. Prepare a good tablespoon of mixed chopped fresh herbs, making your own selection. Parsley, chives, chervil are favourites. Add a touch of lemon thyme, marjoram, or rosemary to accompany meat; fennel or dill for fish. Mix the herbs with 2–3 oz. softened salted butter, according to the size of the loaf. Cut the loaf almost through diagonally in slices $\frac{1}{2}$ inch apart, and spread both sides of each cut with butter. Press the loaf back into shape, wrap in kitchen foil. Place in a hot oven for 12–15 minutes.

Herb Salad Bread

8 OZ. SELF-RAISING FLOUR	3 OZ. FINELY GRATED STRONG
1$\frac{1}{2}$ LEVEL TEASPOONS SALT	CHEDDAR CHEESE
I LEVEL TEASPOON DRY MUSTARD	I EGG, BEATEN
I LEVEL TEASPOON MIXED HERBS	$\frac{1}{4}$ PINT WATER
I TABLESPOON CHOPPED PARSLEY	I OZ. BUTTER OR MARGARINE, MELTED

Sieve flour, salt and mustard together and stir in the mixed herbs, parsley and grated cheese. Add the beaten egg, water and melted fat all at once and stir until blended. Spoon mixture into well greased 1-lb. loaf tin and bake in a moderate oven for about 1 hour. Remove from tin and cool on a wire tray. Serve freshly baked with butter and salad.

Household Uses

Herbs have many medicinal as well as culinary uses. They have long been used to make herb vinegars and herbal teas.

How to make Herb Vinegars: To get the full flavour use fresh plants. Cut the leafy tips just before the plant flowers, pack them loosely into a wide-mouthed jar after bruising the foliage with a wooden potato masher or pestle. Bring either cider or white wine vinegar to boiling point and pour it over the leaves, filling the jar to within two inches of the top. Cover tightly. Let the mixture infuse for ten days in a warm place, shaking the jar about once a day. Taste the vinegar and if it is not strong enough, strain the herbs through a sieve and add another batch of well-bruised herbs to the same liquid without boiling and infuse ten days more. When the vinegar is strong enough, strain the herbs through a sieve and filter the vinegar through muslin, flannel or French filter paper. Store in glass bottles.

Mint Vinegar: When patted on the forehead will relieve a headache. Other herbs commonly used for cooking vinegars are tarragon, mint, burnet, basil, marjoram and dill.

How to make Herbal Teas: The flavours of these teas are usually most delicate and can be very easily impaired by using badly dried or badly packed herbs. The flavours of herbs are also easily affected by metal, therefore they should be infused only in earthenware, china, porcelain or glass. Too long steeping can ruin the flavour, so it is best to steep the leaves a shorter time and rather use more of the herb if a stronger infusion is desired.

If Dried Herbs are used: 1 teaspoon of herbs for each cup and 1 teaspoon for the teapot is considered adequate. **A Tea from Aromatic Seeds:** 1 tablespoon to a pint of water, and the seeds should be crushed well before adding the boiling water.

If Fresh Leaves are used: 3 teaspoons of the herb for each cup is suggested, and the fresh leaves should be bruised by crushing them in a clean cloth before infusing.

Camomile Tea: The popular *tisane* drunk everywhere in France as an aid to digestion after heavy meals. It also relieves nervous headaches. A camomile infusion is excellent as a mouth-wash, as a gargle or for a sore throat.

Verbena Tea: Used as a digestive, to soothe the nerves and as a sedative nightcap. Lemon verbena has a better flavour and it can be blended with mint and taken hot or iced.

Herbs have often been used to flavour either hot or cold China tea, or a sprig of mint or lemon balm is used for iced tea.

Catnip Mice: Cats love catmint as well as mice so that a combination of the two, however approximate, gives them endless amusement. Make the mice from grey flannel or felt. Use grey wool for a tail and whiskers, knotted black thread for eyes. Embroider or draw in the mouth. Stuff with catmint which will give off its fragrance when the cat bites on the cloth.

Herb Incense: Sweet-smelling herbs dried and burned in a room have the same effect as incense, giving an antiseptic fragrance. They can be used to get rid of tobacco, kitchen, or sickroom smells. The leafy tops of lavender, rosemary, sage, lemon balm, etc., may be dried, rubbed through a fine sieve and the powder stored in small, wide-mouthed containers. A little mound of this powdered fragrance readily lights on an incense burner and is most delightful. A handful of sage thrown on an open fire smells good in a stuffy room.

Aromatic Bath Sachets: There are several herbs which have been used for centuries and are still used in the bath for relaxing tired muscles. A simple way of preparing them to put in your bath is to tie a handful in a piece of muslin. Or, if you want to give herb bags as presents, sew neat little square containers of muslin. Drop the bag in the bath while it is being run to allow it to infuse as long as possible and give out its fragrance. Most popular are the mints and thymes, sage, rosemary, camomile flowers, lavender, lemon verbena and lemon balm.

Moth Preventatives: Many combinations of moth repellant mixtures can be made and enclosed in small pads or bags to place among stored clothes or hung on clotheshangers in wardrobes. The following are effective mixtures: A handful each of dried and crumbled thyme, tansy, lemon balm; one tablespoon crushed cloves. Two handfuls each of dried lavender flowers, rosemary; one tablespoon each crushed cloves and small pieces of dried lemon peel.

Inhalation for a Cold: Persistent catarrh can be helped by making an infusion of the following and inhaling it with a towel over the head for 10–15 minutes: a handful of whole or shredded peppermint leaves, whole lime flowers, camomile flowers, or shredded sage leaves. Pour 2–3 pints of boiling water over the herbs. Stay indoors for at least an hour afterwards, or inhale before going to bed.

Hair Rinses: Camomile is good for blonde hair, sage and nettles make a tonic rinse, lime flowers and rosemary are supposed to stimulate growth.

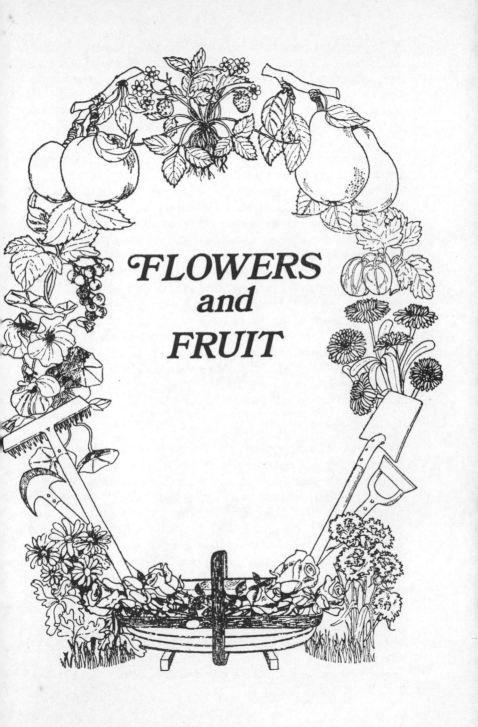

FLOWERS and FRUIT

Flowers have been cultivated for thousands of years, especially, in the Middle and Far East. The Hanging Gardens of Babylon, for instance, were known to have had more than three hundred thousand roses. At the same time flowers were growing wild everywhere. But then, and for many centuries afterwards, they were little valued in this country for their decorative use.

Like herbs, flowers began to be cultivated in Britain for their value in medicinal remedies, for their sweet perfumes to scent the air, and for the many uses they had in cooking. The whole conception of growing them for their beauty came from abroad.

The Romans are known to have had pleasure and herb gardens here, and though there were already many wild roses native to Britain (the dog rose being the best known) they would certainly have brought cultivated varieties, together with other plants they introduced, since the rose was such a favourite in Rome. After discovering new and more exotic varieties of rose in the Middle East, they lost their heads over this flower to such an extent that it became a threat to their economy—instead of growing food, roses were grown—and some early rose species which have been used for hybridising were introduced by the Romans first to France, and later to Britain. When the Romans left this country, for hundreds of years horticulture as an art almost totally disappeared. Many plants like the rose became wild.

Roses of England

The monks who came over from the mainland of Europe from the sixth century onwards to fill the monasteries re-introduced the cultivated rose and brought with them the lily, both symbols of the Virgin Mary, to embellish their altars. The Normans added to these a number of rose species, as well as other flowers, still in cultivation—one being the lovely old Apothecary Rose, *Rosa Gallica*, which became the red rose of the House of Lancaster. Another was *Rosa Alba*, the white rose of York. Chaucer wrote of the Red Cabbage or Provençal Rose. The Crusaders brought back still more roses from the East including the fragrant Damask Rose. As well as its uses in cooking and medicine, the rose was known as one of the six Amulet herbs of Saxon times, in the Middle Ages it was of great religious significance, and the first 'rosaries' were made out of pounded rose petals, moulded into beads and threaded. These gave out a delicious fragrance when clasped in a warm hand.

Another old flower held in great esteem in Saxon times was the Peony. It was used both for flavouring purposes and as a charm against evil.

In Tudor times flowers of all sorts are mentioned. A bill paid by Queen Elizabeth for flowers to welcome the City trained bands who entertained her with a military display is still preserved at Greenwich:

Gely flowers and marygolds	1s 3d
Garland	7d
Strawing herbs	1s 4d
Bowes for the chemneys	1d
Flowers for the potts in the wyndowes	6d

Queen Elizabeth's favourite 'strawing herb' for spreading on the floors was meadowsweet.

Flower Cries

In 1685, at the coronation of James II, the procession was headed by the Royal Herb Woman 'with her six maidens strewing flowers and herbs'. By now flowers were being sold in the streets; rosemary, lavender, thyme, roses, marigolds, myrtle, stock and mignonette were the kind of flowers that the streetseller 'cried'. Many of these melodious cries became well known over the years, such as the haunting 'Sweet smelling lavender, six fine bunches for one penny'. The emphasis was on sweet-smelling flowers and herbs, which were badly needed at times to mask the disagreeable odours caused by bad sanitation. It was during the seventeenth century that pot plants started to be taken indoors, and by the early eighteenth century interior decoration included boughs, wreaths and 'basons' of cut flowers.

In days when paper and ink were rare commodities, and few other than the rich could write at all, love messages were conveyed by sending posies. Many flowers and herbs have a special significance. For example, being given a bunch of rosemary and pansies meant that you were remembered in the sender's loving thoughts.

By Victorian times, the demand for flowers and pot plants had grown, and much of the developing glasshouse industry at the end of the nineteenth century was given over to producing these. Huge glasshouses were erected for the growing of choice blooms. And the season of most kinds of flowers gradually increased until, with

85

flowers such as roses, carnations and, more recently, chrysanthemeums, it became a year-round one.

Floristry as we know it today began about 1850. Before that there was hardly a shop selling flowers in any town in the country. Yet people were flower conscious—particularly fashionable ladies. As : flowers became more used decoratively, they were used less for the old culinary purposes. Many of the old country garden flowers went out of fashion and the highly cultivated varieties were often without perfume, the scent which was so important for flavouring and distilling. Only in humble cottage gardens were the old and traditional varieties kept alive, together with some of the old-fashioned ways of using them, but a lot of flower lore is now regarded sceptically and apart from candied petals, flower waters and oils, flowers are used very little in cooking. The time has surely come for a revival, providing care is used in experimenting with flowers other than these mentioned below, as some may be poisonous.

Flowers used in cooking

Blackcurrant: Corinth, Greece, gave blackcurrants to the world, hence the name. The flowers were used in sweet syrups and confectionary, as well as the fruit so popular today.

Broom Buds: These have an almond flavour and can be pickled as other flower buds and used in similar ways as capers.

Carnation or Clove Pink: The name carnation is supposed to derive from coronation, because this was the flower traditionally used to make floral wreaths and crowns for great festivals. The petals of clove carnations or 'gillyflowers' (probably derived from 'July flower') were used in even more ways than were rose petals. Wine was flavoured with them, and the flowers also candied, pickled, made into conserves, and served up in sauce to eat with mutton, up to the end of the eighteenth century. This was, of course, the pink, not the cultivated carnation grown today.

Cowslips: They can be candied, made into syrups, vinegars, etc., put into butters as other flowers. They have an odour of anise and are supposed to have soporific powers.

Dandelion: Although a weed, is credited with great health-giving powers. The flowers are used to make wine, the leaves in salads, and a kind of coffee substitute is made from the root. The leaves which are coarsely serrated like jagged saws, are supposed to resemble the canine teeth of a lion, hence the old French name *dent-de-lion*, and our own dandelion.

Elder: The elder tree provides food, drink and medicine, and the same properties are found in every part of it. The flowers made into fritters, when they are just opening, are delicious. Country people used to make a pickle from the blossoms, and another kind from tender young elder shoots, and the berries went into ketchup and chutney. Excellent wines are made from both the flowers and elderberries. Many medicinal uses are described later in this chapter.

Marigold: Uses include seasoning, colouring for butter, and a replacement for saffron. Marigold petals can be used fresh or dried, in salads, braised beef, chowders, chicken soup, and broths. The secret of the famous Dutch soups' rich colour and flavour, was the use of the marigold. Medieval French and English cooks liked it too. (Do not confuse with French or African marigolds.)

Marsh Mallow: Boiled in wine or milk, marsh mallow was once a popular remedy for coughs, bronchitis and similar troubles, and the Romans esteemed the marsh mallow as a succulent vegetable. In France the fresh young tops are still put into salads. The roots, when first boiled and then fried with onions and butter, are said to form a palatable dish which has often been valuable in times of food shortage.

Nasturtium: One of the classics, for it fulfils the requirements of any gardener; it has fragrance and beauty in the garden and many uses in the kitchen. Its name results from its pungent odour, for 'nasturtium' comes from the words *nasus* (nose) and *torquere* (to twist)—the 'nose twister'—describing its ability to make the nostril quiver and twist.

Pansy: This is another old flower, which is supposed to symbolise loving thoughts. It can be made into a wine, used for decoration as violets and roses, the petals candied and crystallised, etc.

Peony: It is considered an omen of good fortune. The ground seeds were used as pepper in the Middle Ages.

Primrose: The name of this early-blooming spring flower comes from medieval Latin *prima rosa*, meaning the first rose. In cooking its flavour is similar to the cowslip. The petals or whole flowers can be crystallised.

Rose: Believed to be the oldest plant found in the modern garden, it has many uses and many legends attached to it. The rose was plucked on Midsummer Eve, and if it had not faded by the beginning of July, maidens knew their lovers were faithful.

The red rose became red because the tears of Venus, when she lost Adonis, fell on the white rose and turned it crimson.

For recipes use the old-fashioned perfumed roses, the more fragrant the better, such as these:

White varieties—Queen of Denmark, Great Maiden's Blush.
Red varieties—Belle de Crécy, Cardinal Richelieu.
Damask (especially fragrant)—Gloire de Guilan, Madame Hardy.

Rose-Geranium or Scented Leaf Geranium: A large branching plant with inconspicuous flowers but fragrant, deeply cut leaves. The dried leaves are a delightful addition to potpourri. The fresh or dried leaves can give a delicate flavour to many sweets, jams and jellies and fruit cups, or used to line cake tins.

Sunflower: Long before the coming of the white man and the exploitation of sunflower-oil, the American Indians were using the seeds of the larger species of sunflowers as important sources of food; they serve in making bread, cakes and rich soups. It was said by explorers that the roasted seeds were used in preparing a drink 'tasting just like coffee'.

Violets: Wood violets grow wild in most parts of Europe including Britain. The sweet violet has probably been cultivated in Britain since gardens began. It has many of the same uses as the rose.

FRUIT

Although wild fruits such as apples, plums, gooseberries and currants were certainly picked and eaten, fruit was not cultivated in Britain until the Romans came. The Romans are generally given credit for introducing the orchard as well as the herb and vegetable garden. The orchard (fruit trees grown together in a group near a farmhouse) was almost certainly a Roman innovation.

Most of our popular cultivated fruits can still be found growing in a wild state. The earliest kinds of apples were mainly of the crab apple varieties, and were used for cider. If a particular kind of cider apple was sweet enough it was no doubt eaten, especially by children who, as today, knew which varieties of cider apple were good to eat. Apples were valued primarily as the basis of potent drinks. But no one bothered then about cultivating them especially for eating.

The wassailing of apple trees to make them fruitful, a ritual carried out in the West Country until recent times, was of pagan origin. In the Welsh, Cornish and Irish languages the apple is 'avall' or 'aball', and the early inhabitants of Somerset ranked it so high that their town, which stood on the site of present-day Glastonbury, was known as Avallonia or 'apple orchard'. The making of perry from pears is also a very old practice dating back at least to the third century.

As the medieval era drew to a close, greater communication with the Continent began to influence fruit growing. The Normans would have brought new varieties of fruit with them once they had settled down after the 1066 invasion, for Normandy was then well ahead of Britain in fruit culture.

Both cider apples and perry pears were important crops in the West Country from the Norman Conquest onwards. Over on the east side of England, fruit growing was subject to influences from the Continent from an early date. Plums and cherries were also eaten, though, until the sixteenth century, most of the choice dessert varieties would have been imported.

By 1300, apples were beginning to be given names such as pear-main and costard; pearmain seems to have been a general name but the costard was a particularly large apple and possibly a definite variety. It is from the word 'costard' that costermonger—seller of costards—derives. Wild strawberries and raspberries were beginning to be transplanted into gardens and the sweeter varieties cultivated.

In the time of Henry VIII, fruit was enjoyed both as a dessert and for cooking, the best having still to be brought in from the Continent and therefore much too expensive for the ordinary person. The aristocracy began to bring in trees for planting in their private gardens but it was Henry himself who first encouraged the growing of fruit on a commercial scale. Orchards contained both trees and bushes; cherries, apricots, apples, pears, peaches, nectarines, bullaces, damsons and plums growing in picturesque confusion with gooseberries and red currants. Barberries and whortleberries were also cultivated. It was not until a later date that fruit bushes were sited more in the vegetable section of the kitchen garden.

Apples were always the most important fruit in Britain, as roses were the most important flowers. Besides being extensively used for eating, cooking and making cider, they were also in favour at one time as a cosmetic. Gerard, in his *Herball*, says they were used to soften the skin and take away freckles. To the pulp of cooked apples was added rose water and 'swine's grease', the resulting concoction being sold under the name of pomatum. Even in those early days their value against scurvy was realised, and barrels of apples were taken to sea by sailors going on long voyages, to supplement their diet.

Fruit culture expands

It was during the seventeenth century that fruit-growing on a commercial scale became well established in Britain, and from then on British fruit was able to hold its own against all comers. Early in that century Busoni, Chaplain to the Venetian Ambassador, wrote: 'The apples are really very good and cheap, of various sorts and procurable all the year round. The pears are scarcely eatable and the other fruits most abominable, their taste resembling that of grass. The numerous sorts of cherries and egriots which one sees in Italy may well be desired in this kingdom, though certainly not enjoyed, for generally in the markets they sell one single sort of very bad morella. Yet the English are extremely greedy of them, especially the women, buying them at the beginning of the season in bunches at the cost of an eye!'

During the next hundred years or so the profession of nurseryman developed considerably. Still more plants were coming in from abroad. The modern large red strawberry, for example, was evolved from varieties introduced from Carolina and from China by way of Holland.

The buying and selling of plants (flowers as well as fruit) had always taken place in a small way at local markets, but now became more of a specialised trade. A small nurseryman supplied the owners of modest kitchen and pleasure gardens with a large variety of seeds, seedlings and young trees. A man in a bigger way of business coped as well with the more exotic requirements of the wealthy. As time went on, owners of large properties began to take a pride in their orangeries, then their greenhouse and even hothouse produce. This cult reached its zenith in the Victorian conservatory, where tropical plants and birds flourished. Country folk, of course, exchanged cuttings of the more successful varieties, like cherished recipes, with relatives and friends, and still do.

BLACKCURRANT

Ice Sorbet from Buds of Flowers: An unusual and delicately flavoured ice sorbet can be made from the buds of black currant flowers. Make a sugar syrup with a pint of water and 8 oz. sugar and simmer 4 oz. of black currant flower buds in it for 10 minutes. Add the juice of half a lemon. Strain. Freeze in the freezing compartment of the refrigerator. Stir well, then return to refrigerator.

Blackcurrant Leaves: The leaves of blackcurrant bushes can be gathered in early summer, dried and rubbed down, and be used to make a tea, or added to an Indian blend to make it go further.

CARNATION OR CLOVE PINK

Clove Carnation Syrup: Pick off the husks and chop off the white ends of sweet-smelling carnation heads, and measure 3 pints of flower petals. Pour five pints of boiling water over these. Leave to stand for 12 hours. Strain off the liquid without pressing, and dissolve 2 lb. of sugar to every pint in this. Bottle and keep until required. Use as a sauce for puddings and to flavour fruit dishes and drinks.

Marmalade of Carnations

8 OZ. FRESH RED CARNATION PETALS	8 OZ. SUGAR $\frac{1}{2}$ PINT WATER

Crush the petals well. Boil together the sugar and water to make a strong syrup. Add the crushed flowers and simmer in the syrup until they become a pulp. Stir well and store in small jars.

Carnation Jelly: Make up a pint of jelly—raspberry jelly combines well with carnation. Pour half an inch of jelly into a rinsed mould, let it set, then place a layer of carnation flower heads (with green husks trimmed off) on this. Pour more jelly over these, carefully, then more flower petals, layer upon layer until the mould is full. Allow to set. This jelly looks delicious when unmoulded.

Carnation Butter: Pound heavily some strongly scented carnation petals and mix well into some butter. Serve spread on toasted bread shapes and garnish each with a fresh carnation petal.

COWSLIP

Pickled Cowslips: Wash and dry the freshly picked flowers. Remove the green calyxes at the bottom. To each pound of flowers allow 1 lb. of sugar and 1 pint of white wine vinegar. Boil all to a syrup. Put into dry, warm jars and seal.

Flavouring Cakes: Use either fresh or dried cowslip flower heads (with green base) in cakes as a flavouring instead of fruit, etc. Primrose petals can be used in the same manner, their flavour is similar.

Note: Cowslip flower heads can be candied in the same way as primroses; a syrup can be made using the recipe for pansies and they make a good flavoured butter (see recipe using carnations).

DANDELION

Dandelion Shrub: Wash 2 quarts of blossoms. Pour on them 1 gallon of boiling water. Let it stand overnight, strain through double muslin, add juice of 3 lemons and 4 lb. granulated sugar. Heat until sugar is dissolved. Strain and bottle in airtight bottles. Serve in glasses with a little chipped ice. A delicious, healthful drink.

ELDER

Gooseberry jelly: The flavour of elder flowers combines well with gooseberries and it is a good and old custom to put elderflower in the jars before pouring in freshly made gooseberry jelly preserve.

93

Elderflower Fritters: The flower heads can be made into fritters, either as for rose fritters or dipped in a thin batter, fried and sprinkled with caster sugar.

Elderflower and Gooseberry Water Ice: Make a syrup by dissolving 5 lb. of sugar in 2 pints of water. Add 1½ lb. topped and tailed gooseberries and cook gently for 5 minutes. Tie a one-pint measure of elderflower heads in a piece of muslin or bag, put into the syrup and let it soak for 6 hours. Remove flowers and pour mixture into a pan for freezing. Freeze, then beat well. Put back into freezer to freeze again until required.

LAVENDER

Lavender Tea: A fragrant and unusual flavoured tea can be made with the young leaves. Pour a pint of boiling water on a level tablespoon of these and allow to infuse for 2–3 minutes. Serve hot or iced.

Lavender Jelly: To vary the flavour of apple jelly preserve, put some lavender flowers in the bottom of the jars. Pour in the apple jelly while it is hot. Seal in the usual way, while hot, for storing.

MARIGOLD

For Buns and Cakes: Fill a small muslin bag with marigold petals and soak this in a small cup of hot milk. The milk can then be used for mixing in cakes, puddings and even custards to give a new flavour.

Scrambled Eggs with Marigolds: Beat up 4 eggs with 4 tablespoons of milk. Flavour to taste with salt, pepper and nutmeg. Heat in a tablespoon of melted butter. Scramble the egg mixture in this. When almost cooked add petals of 2 marigolds which have been washed and chopped. Serve on toast and garnish with more marigold petals.

Marigold Custard: Bruise a half-pint measure of marigold petals and pour a pint of warm milk flavoured with vanilla over them. Add the lightly beaten yolks of 3 eggs, 4 oz. sugar, a pinch of salt and a good bunch of both nutmeg and allspice. Cook gently until it begins to thicken, then add a teaspoon of rose water. Cook in a warm oven until set. Serve with whipped cream and decorate with marigold petals.

Marigold Rice: Fry lightly a finely chopped onion in a tablespoon of vegetable oil. Add 8 oz. rice and fry for 3 minutes. Pour in a pint of vegetable stock. Add salt to taste and some freshly chopped or dried rosemary. Stir in 3 teaspoons of bruised marigold petals. Cook until rice is tender, about 10 minutes. Leave covered for rice to soak up liquid. Serve instead of potatoes sprinkled with grated cheese and little dots of butter.

MARSH MALLOW

Marsh mallows: Today these sweets are made with gelatine, refined sugar, flavouring, etc., but they were originally made from the dried, powdered roots of the marsh mallow plant. About 2 oz. of this powder was mixed with 14 oz. finely crushed sugar. This was bound together with a little gum tragacanth and orange flower water. It was then shaped into balls and left to dry.

Mallow Soup: The young leaves can be used in the same way as spinach for a soup, or they can be included with other vegetables when making a green vegetable soup.

NASTURTIUM

Everything but the root is used in cooking. The young tender stems and leaves are extremely succulent in salads, the chopped young leaves are very tasty in sandwiches, the blossoms enhance fruit salads, and minced blossoms can be blended into creamed butter or cheese for use as a spread. The unripe and still green seeds with their peppery taste are a favourite part of the plant and are used as substitutes for the more exotic capers. The unopened flower buds are also peppery and can be used in many dishes.

Try a single seed in a cup of tea!

Try sliced pears decorated with nasturtium flowers.

Mix nasturtium flowers with butter or cream cheese and spread on a fruit bread.

Nasturtium leaves contain 10 times as much Vitamin C as lettuce.

Nasturtium Sauce: 'Take a quart of nasturtium flowers and pour over a quart of vinegar, in which has been boiled for 10 minutes 6 shallots, 6 cloves, a teaspoon salt, and ½ teaspoon pepper. Keep the flowers covered with this mixture for a month and then strain into bottles.' (A Victorian recipe.)

Sauce for Cold Lamb: Make a thick white sauce with 2 oz. butter, 2 oz. flour, ¾ pint milk, 2 tablespoons chopped nasturtium seeds.

Nasturtium Soup: Heat 2 pints of chicken stock, add 8 tablespoons nasturtium blossoms fried in butter, salt and pepper to taste. Serve hot.

Pickled Nasturtium Seeds

1 LB. NASTURTIUM SEEDS	1 QUART WHITE WINE VINEGAR
4 WHOLE CLOVES	1 TEASPOON SALT
2 BLADES MACE	

Put seeds, cloves and mace in an earthenware jar. Bring vinegar and salt to boiling point and pour over seeds. Cover the crock tightly. Let it stand for 1 month before using.

Nasturtium Salad

1 SMALL ROUND LETTUCE	A FEW GREEN NASTURTIUM
¼ TEASPOON SALT	SEEDS (OPTIONAL)
½ TEASPOON SUGAR	8 OZ. SMALL NEW POTATOES,
1 TEASPOON FRENCH MUSTARD	COOKED AND SLICED
2 TABLESPOONS WHITE WINE	8 NASTURTIUM FLOWERS
VINEGAR	5 NASTURTIUM LEAVES AND
4 TABLESPOONS SINGLE CREAM	STALKS

Wash and dry lettuce, and break up larger leaves. Make a dressing with the seasonings, vinegar and cream and the chopped seeds. Put potatoes, mixed with 3 nasturtium flowers roughly chopped, in a salad bowl. Pour over the dressing. Arrange on top of the potatoes. Space out the 5 nasturtium leaves round the edge of the bowl with a flower head arranged on top of each leaf. To serve, lightly toss all salad ingredients together.

PANSY

Pansy Jelly: Make a lemon jelly and after pouring a little of it into the mould, place a purple pansy flower in it, face downwards. Carefully pour in the rest of the jelly. When the jelly is turned out it will be face side up. Pretty to see and it also adds a subtle flavour.

Pansy Flower Syrup: Take about a pint measure of pansy flowers, cover with water and let simmer for 2 or 3 hours. To keep in fragrance the pan must be tightly covered. Strain and add 1 lb. sugar to each pint of liquid.

PEONY

Peony Kernels: These were used dried and powdered as a pepper or condiment with food in the Middle Ages. They have a piquant flavour and can be used in cooking or to decorate cakes and desserts in the same way as sliced almonds are used.

Peony Water: This was a popular drink in the seventeenth and eighteenth centuries, and also thought to have some health-giving qualities. Make it by infusing two pint measures of peony flowers (without any green calyx) in wine to cover for 24 hours. Remove the flowers from the wine and boil them up with 2 pints of water. Simmer for 5–10 minutes. Strain the liquid off and sweeten it to taste with sugar or honey. Add the peony water to the wine.

D

PRIMROSE

Primrose Salad: It is well known that the primrose was Disraeli's favourite flower, and it was used as the emblem of the Primrose League he founded, but it is not generally known that he also ate them. The young shoots of the plants were picked and soaked in salt water for a few minutes, then drained and boiled in water to cover for 10 minutes. A vinaigrette sauce was poured over the well drained shoots, and primrose petals decorated the dish.

Primrose Fritters: Heat some butter in a pan and cook primrose flower heads in this until slightly browned. Serve hot with sugar and orange juice. The flowers can also be cooked in a thin batter.

Candied Primroses: Pick some primroses and remove the green calyxes from the flowers. If damp dry them in a warm oven with the door open. Make a strong sugar syrup cooking it gently until a little dropped in cold water becomes brittle. Put in the primrose heads for a minute. Remove and dry them on a sieve in a warm place. When quite dry sprinkle with icing sugar. Gently open the flowers and sift any extra sugar from them. Store in a dry place.

Primrose Pottage

2 OZ. PUDDING RICE	2 TABLESPOONS PRIMROSE
1 PINT MILK	PETALS
2 TABLESPOONS HONEY	$\frac{1}{4}$ TEASPOON CINNAMON
2 OZ. GROUND ALMONDS	$\frac{1}{2}$ OZ. BUTTER

Put the rice in an ovenproof dish, pour in the milk. Stir in the honey and ground almonds. Bruise some of the petals with a wooden spoon and mix them in with the rice and milk. Add cinnamon, dot with butter and cook in slow oven until set. Serve sprinkled with fresh petals.

ROSES

There are more recipes using roses than for any other flower, and unlike many another flower that was once used in cooking the rose is still used a lot in different parts of the world. The old-fashioned perfumed variety of rose—the more fragrant the better—is necessary for the recipes given.

Rose Fritters: Dip rose petals first in brandy, then into melted butter and fry in deep fat. Serve dusted with caster sugar.

Candied Rose Petals: There are two ways to candy petals, one cold, the other hot. (1) Brush the petals with white of egg mixed with a little water. Sprinkle them thoroughly with granulated sugar and leave spread out on waxed paper to dry. (2) Dip the petals in rose water in which some gum arabic has been steeped. Sprinkle sugar over them and dry in the lowest of oven temperatures. Store candied petals in a box with a tight lid, arranged on waxed paper so that they do not touch. Put a layer of waxed paper between layers of petals.

Honey of Roses: Mash a half-pint of rose petals which have had the white ends cut off, with a wooden spoon or masher. Boil them for 15 minutes in a pint of water. Add 2 lb. of clear honey and boil down gently to a thick syrup. Pour into sterilised glass jars and seal for storing.

Turkish Rose Petal Jam: Chop off the white ends of about 30 large red cabbage roses (or some other sweet-scented variety). Dissolve 3 lb. sugar in 2 pints water. Add juice of half a lemon and the rose petals. Boil slowly until the roses crystallise, stirring frequently with a wooden spoon.

Rose Mousse: Beat 6 egg whites until stiff and peaky. Gradually add rose petal jam to taste. Fold in 2 tablespoons of brandy (fruit flavoured or rose brandy) and pour into a soufflé dish. Put into a hot oven, leave for 10 minutes or until set.

Rose Brandy: Add about a pint measure of heavily perfumed rose petals to 2 pints of brandy. Allow to stand for a month, then make a syrup with 1 lb. sugar and $1\frac{1}{4}$ pints of water. Boil and add another pint measure of petals to this. Simmer for an hour. Strain and mix with the strained brandy. Bottle for storing.

Pickled Rosebuds: Pick about 40 tight rosebuds, and wash well.

Place in a 2-pint jar. Mix 4 oz. sugar with 1 pint of white wine vinegar; pour over the rosebuds. Seal the jar with wax and store in a warm, dry place for at least a month. Pickled buds can then be used in salads, with cold meat, or in sandwiches.

Rose Petal Water Ice: Take 2 pints of water, 1 lb. sugar, 2 teaspoons of finely grated lemon rind, ¼ pint lemon juice, 2 tablespoons rose petal jam and mix well together. Bring to the boil, stirring. Allow to cool, then freeze. Beat, and return to freezer until required.

Rose Petals in Pies: It is an old country custom to strew a handful of fragrant rose petals under the crust of a cherry or plum pie. Dark red roses impart the most flavour.

ROSE-GERANIUM

Rose-Geranium Jelly

½ PINT ROSE-GERANIUM LEAVES
2½ LB. SUGAR
1 TEASPOON WHOLE ALLSPICE
JUICE 2 LEMONS

2 PINTS WATER
½ BOTTLE COMMERCIAL PECTIN
FEW DROPS RED FOOD
  COLOURING

Wash the leaves well. Pat fairly dry. Mix them with the sugar, allspice and lemon juice and leave for 1 hour at least. Put in a saucepan, add the water and bring to the boil. Strain, add the pectin to the liquid, boil again, stirring, for 1–2 minutes. Add the food colouring for desired shade of pink. Pour into small jars for storing, each with a rose-geranium leaf inside. Seal.

Rose-Geranium Punch

2 PINTS APPLE JUICE
8 OZ. SUGAR
6 ROSE-GERANIUM LEAVES

4 LIMES OR 2 LEMONS
6 DROPS GREEN FOOD
  COLOURING

Bring to the boil the apple juice with the sugar and leaves added. Simmer for 5 minutes. Add the limes or lemons, thinly sliced and crushed. Cool, strain and add the colouring. Serve poured into glasses half filled with cracked ice and each garnished with a rose-geranium leaf.

Rose-Geranium Tea: An infusion of the leaves makes a delicately rose-flavoured drink and can be served hot or iced. A crushed leaf at the bottom of a cup can be used as a flavouring in ordinary tea or herb teas.

VIOLET

Violet Syrup

2 PINTS VIOLET FLOWERS $2\frac{1}{2}$ PINTS WATER
  (WITHOUT GREEN CALYX)   SUGAR

Put washed flowers in a china crock. Bring the water to the boil and pour over flowers. Allow to stand for 24 hours. Strain through muslin. Measure, return to pan and add twice as much sugar as liquid. Heat to dissolve but do not boil. Bottle to store.

Violet Soufflé

2 OZ. BUTTER   3 EGG YOLKS
2 OZ. FLOUR   3 EGG WHITES
$\frac{1}{2}$ PINT MILK   4 OZ. CANDIED VIOLETS
1 TABLESPOON CHERRY BRANDY   CANDIED VIOLETS TO DECORATE
2 TABLESPOONS SUGAR

Heat the butter and mix in the flour, stirring well for 2 minutes. Remove from heat and stir in milk, then heat until thick and smooth. Cool. Beat cherry brandy, sugar and egg yolks together.

Stir into the sauce. Beat the egg whites until stiff and peaky. Fold into the sauce together with chopped, candied violets. Pour mixture into a soufflé dish, bake in a moderately hot oven until a light brown. Serve decorated with more candied violets.

Violet Ice Cream: Crush 2 oz. candied violets with a rolling pin, between folds of a tea towel. Put in a basin with 4 oz. demerara sugar and 4 oz. soft brown breadcrumbs. Gradually fold in 1 pint whipped cream. Freeze until firm, beat and freeze again.

Note: The rather coarse sugar produces the unusually delicious texture and flavour of this ice cream.

Candied Violets: These are made in the same way as for rose petals.

Violet Vinegar: Put in a jar a well-packed half-pint measure of fragrant violet flowers (without stems or green calyx). Cover with wine vinegar, cork and allow to stand for two weeks in the sun or a warm place. Strain through muslin. Fill bottles and cork well to store, but can be used immediately. A tablespoon in a glass of iced water, sweetened with honey, makes a most soothing drink.

A Banquet Salad: Mix 1 lb. of cold, diced potatoes with 8 oz. unpeeled, diced dessert apples. Make a vinaigrette dressing with 4 tablespoons olive oil, 2 tablespoons lemon juice, with salt and coarsely ground pepper to taste. Pour this over the potato mixture. Fold in a tablespoon violet flowers (without stem or calyx). Decorate with finely chopped green pepper or finely chopped hard-boiled egg and a few more flower heads.

Flower vinegars

In the old days and until the middle nineteenth century, flower vinegars such as rose, violet, clove pink, elder flower, lavender and rosemary were very popular, not only for toilet preparations but also for salads and iced beverages.

Making Flower Vinegars: Collect a cupful of petals, cut off the white bases, put the petals into a wide-mouthed jar, add a pint of boiling white vinegar and cover tightly. Let the mixture infuse for 10 days in a warm place, shaking the jar about once a day. Taste the vinegar, and if it is not strong enough, strain the flowers through a sieve, and add another charge of petals to the same liquid without boiling and infuse 10 days more. When the vinegar is strong enough, strain the flowers through a sieve, and filter the vinegar through muslin. Store in glass bottles.

Sometimes instead of one flower alone, a combination or bouquet vinegar is made for toilet use, such as these:

1. One part lavender flower petals, 4 parts fragrant red rose petals.
2. Equal parts clove pinks, rose petals, rosemary and elder flowers.

APPLES

Huntingdon Fidget Pie

I LB. COOKING APPLES	SALT AND PEPPER TO TASTE
8 OZ. ONIONS	8 OZ. SHORTCRUST PASTRY
12 OZ. STREAKY BACON	

Peel, core and slice apples. Put a layer at the bottom of a pie dish. On top of apples, place a layer of sliced onions, followed by a layer of diced bacon. Repeat until dish is full adding to each layer a sprinkling of salt and pepper. Add a very little water, cover with a thick pastry crust, and bake in a moderate oven for 2 hours.

Apple Marigold

3 LARGE COOKING APPLES	I TEASPOON THYME
2 EGGS	I TEASPOON SAGE
½ PINT MILK	I SMALL PEPPERCORN, GROUND
I TEASPOON MARIGOLD PETALS	BUTTER

Peel and core apples and cut in rings. Beat the eggs and milk, season with the marigold, chopped thyme and sage, and peppercorn. Put egg mixture in a shallow dish, place apple rings on top and dot with butter. Bake in a moderately hot oven for 20–25 minutes.

Apple Bread: A light and pleasant bread is made with a mixture of apples and flour in proportion 1 lb. apples to 2 lb. flour. The usual quantity of yeast is required as in making ordinary bread, and is mixed with the flour and warm apple pulp (they have been peeled, cored and cooked with very little water and sugar, if required, to taste). The dough is allowed to rise for 3–4 hours, then baked in bread tins for 1–1¼ hours in a moderately hot oven.

Somerset Apple Dice: Peel, core and dice 2 large cooking apples, and turn them in caster sugar before they discolour. Cut 2 thick slices stale bread into cubes the same size. Melt about 1 oz. of butter in a thick frying pan, and fry the sugared dice quickly, stirring to prevent them from sticking. Add a little more butter and stir in the bread dice, until all are crisp and brown. Serve sifted with powdered cinnamon or nutmeg. Apples which form a pulp easily are not suitable, and a good result can be obtained by using large green-skinned dessert apples, such as Golden Delicious when not too ripe.

Apple Soup: Simmer 2 lb. apples, cut up but not peeled or cored, in 2–2½ pints good stock. When apples are soft press though a strainer. Season with ¼ teaspoon ginger, salt to taste, and reheat with a handful of pearl barley and cook gently until barley is soft.

Apple Marmalade Charlotte

8 OZ. THIN SLICES BREAD AND BUTTER	1 EGG
	1 PINT MILK
2 OZ. MARMALADE	SUGAR TO TASTE
1 LB. COOKING APPLES	

Put a layer of bread into a greased pie dish and cover with a little marmalade and layer of sliced, peeled apple. Cover with bread. Fill the dish in this way, adding sugar to taste, and finishing with a layer of bread. Beat up egg in milk and pour over. Bake in a moderate oven for 30–35 minutes.

Apple Tansy

3 LARGE COOKING APPLES	SUGAR TO TASTE
2 OZ. BUTTER	½ TEASPOON MIXED SPICE
3 EGGS	8 OZ. FINE BREADCRUMBS
1 PINT MILK	

Peel and slice the apples, cook gently in the butter until soft, and pour into a greased fireproof dish. Beat the eggs, add them to the milk and sweeten to taste, add mixed spice. Pour over breadcrumbs and beat lightly, then add all the mixture to the apples and bake slowly until set. Serve with blackberry syrup. (Sliced rhubarb can be used instead of apples to make Rhubarb Tansy.)

Toffee Apples

SMALL APPLES
SKEWERS OR SMOOTH STICKS
4 OZ. BUTTER

8 OZ. TREACLE
I LB. SUGAR
I TABLESPOON VINEGAR

Wash apples and stick them on skewers or sticks. Melt the butter, add treacle to it and the sugar and vinegar. Boil 20 minutes and test for setting, dip in apples and stand on a greased tray.

Note: Have ready a larger saucepan or heatproof bowl of very hot water. Stand the pan in this while dipping the apples so that the toffee will not set too quickly.

Apple Amber

4 OZ. SUGAR
3 OZ. BUTTER
RIND AND JUICE I LEMON

2 LB. COOKING APPLES
3 EGGS
3 TABLESPOONS CASTER SUGAR

Put sugar, butter, juice and grated rind of lemon into a saucepan with the peeled and sliced apples. Simmer until tender, then beat to a purée with a fork or in a blender. Beat up egg yolks and add to purée. Put into a deep greased fireproof dish, and cook in a very slow oven for 20–30 minutes. Whip egg whites stiffly, fold in caster sugar, and put the meringue mixture on top of pudding. Put in moderately hot oven for 10 minutes to brown meringue.

Spicy Apple Crumble

1½ LB. COOKING APPLES	4 OZ. BROWN SUGAR
2 TABLESPOONS BROWN SUGAR	4 OZ. BUTTER
1 TEASPOON GROUND CINNAMON	2 TEASPOONS CORIANDER
8 OZ. FLOUR	SEED, CRUSHED

Peel, core and slice the apples and put into a well-buttered, ovenproof dish. Sprinkle with the sugar and cinnamon. Rub the flour, 4 oz. sugar and butter together until crumbly. Press this mixture down on top of the apples and sprinkle with the coriander. Bake in a moderately hot oven for about 30 minutes. Delicious served hot with cream.

Apple Pie with Cinnamon Crust

8 OZ. SELF-RAISING FLOUR	A LITTLE MILK
1 TABLESPOON ALLSPICE	1½ LB. COOKING APPLES,
3 TEASPOONS CINNAMON	PEELED AND CHOPPED
PINCH SALT	2 TABLESPOONS LEMON JUICE
4 OZ. BROWN SUGAR	4 OZ. SUGAR
4 OZ. BUTTER	WHITE OF EGG FOR GLAZING
1 EGG, BEATEN	

To make pastry, sift flour, spices and salt together. Mix in the sugar, and rub in the butter. Moisten with the egg to a manageable dough, adding a little milk if necessary. Roll out just over half to line a pie plate or ovenproof dish. Mix the chopped apple with lemon juice and sugar and put in the lined dish. Cover with pastry lid, damping edges and pressing down to seal. Flute edges with end of spoon. Brush with white of egg to glaze. Bake in moderate oven for 35–40 minutes.

Note: Instead of apples, the pie may be filled with plums, blackcurrants or gooseberries. With other fruits, add about 4 tablespoons of water.

APRICOTS

Gammon and Apricot Pie

1 LARGE GAMMON RASHER,	1 OZ. SULTANAS
1 INCH THICK	A LITTLE STOCK
1 LB. STONED APRICOTS	1 LB. POTATOES
PEPPER	

Lightly brown the rasher on both sides. Put in a large pie dish. Place apricots on top. Sprinkle with a little pepper, add the sultanas, pour over sufficient stock to cover, then add the peeled and sliced potatoes. Cover lightly with greased greaseproof paper, and bake in a moderate oven for 1 hour. Serve hot.

BLACKBERRIES

Blackberry Honeycomb

1 LB. BLACKBERRIES	½ PINT MILK
3 TEASPOONS GELATINE	3 TABLESPOONS SUGAR
2 TABLESPOONS WATER	

Cook blackberries in a little water, then strain through a sieve, make up the juice to ½ pint if insufficient. Soak gelatine in water and melt in a basin over hot water. Add milk to juice and sugar, bring to blood heat. Add gelatine and stir well until mixture curdles, but do not boil. Pour into a damp mould and leave to set. When turned into a dish it should be a deep purple clear jelly at the bottom with mauve curdled mixture at the top.

Blackberry and Apple Pie

1½ LB. COOKING APPLES, PEELED	8 OZ. BLACKBERRIES
AND CHOPPED	8 OZ. FLAKY PASTRY
2 TABLESPOONS CLEAR HONEY	YOLK OF EGG FOR GLAZING
GOOD PINCH GROUND CLOVES	

Put the chopped apple in a deep pie dish, with a pie funnel in the centre if preferred. (As no water is added this is not strictly necessary.) Add the honey, ground cloves and blackberries. Cover the dish with a layer of pastry, rolled out about ½ inch thick, trim, knock up the edges, and use the trimmings to make decorations.

Pierce the pastry with a fine skewer in the centre to allow steam to escape. Brush with egg yolk moistened with a little water to make a rich golden glaze. Bake in a hot oven for the first 20 minutes, then reduce to moderately hot for a further 20 minutes.

Blackberry Pickle

1 QUART BLACKBERRIES	2 LB. SUGAR
$\frac{1}{2}$ OZ. GINGER, GROUND	$1\frac{1}{2}$ OZ. ALLSPICE
1 PINT WHITE VINEGAR	

Mix the blackberries with the ginger, leave for 12 hours. Bring the vinegar to the boil. Add the berries and sugar and boil for 30 minutes. When cold add the allspice. Mix well, put into jars and cover.

Blackberry Cordial: Pour 1 pint of white wine vinegar over 1 quart of ripe blackberries. Let it stand in an earthenware jar for 7–8 days, stirring meanwhile to extract the juices. Strain off when ready, and put the liquor in an enamel saucepan with 1 lb. loaf sugar and 8 oz. honey. Bring to the boil, then remove from the heat and allow to cool. Bottle and cork and keep in a dark place. 1 tablespoon in a glass of hot water is a pleasant bedtime drink, excellent winter remedy for colds and sore throats.

Blackberry Syrup: Stew the blackberries with $\frac{1}{4}$ pint water to every 3 lb. fruit, until the juice is drawn. Strain, and for every pint of juice add 6 oz. sugar. Boil sugar and juice together for 15 minutes and when cold bottle for use.

CHERRIES

Cherry Soup

1 LB. STONED CHERRIES	1 TABLESPOON ARROWROOT
2 PINTS COLD WATER	JUICE $\frac{1}{2}$ LEMON
4 OZ. CASTER SUGAR	1 TABLESPOON CHERRY BRANDY

Simmer the cherries in the water with the sugar until tender. Pass the mixture through a sieve and return it to the saucepan. Mix the arrowroot with a little cold water, add to the pan and cook for 8–10 minutes. Allow to cool, add lemon juice and brandy. Chill before serving.

Kentish Cherry Batter

$\frac{1}{2}$ LB. RIPE, STONED CHERRIES	$\frac{1}{2}$ PINT MILK
2 TABLESPOONS BROWN SUGAR	8 OZ. FLOUR
4 EGG YOLKS	4 EGG WHITES

Put stoned cherries with sugar on top into a buttered pudding basin. Beat egg yolks with milk, then beat in flour till creamy; let it stand. Whip the egg whites to a stiff froth and fold into the batter. Pour into pudding basin, cover with a cloth or foil and steam for $1\frac{1}{2}$ hours. Serve with extra sugar if liked.

Cherry Meringue Pie

8 OZ. CHERRIES	$\frac{1}{2}$ TEASPOON BAKING POWDER
LITTLE SUGAR	2 EGG YOLKS
6 OZ. SHORTCRUST PASTRY	1 TABLESPOON MILK
2 OZ. BUTTER	$\frac{1}{2}$ TEASPOON VANILLA ESSENCE
2 OZ. SUGAR	2 EGG WHITES
2 OZ. FLOUR	2 TABLESPOONS CASTER SUGAR

Stew cherries with a little sugar and small amount of water, keeping them whole. Line a pie dish with shortcrust pastry. Pour in the cherries. Cream butter and sugar together. Add flour and baking powder alternately, with the beaten egg yolks mixed with milk. Mix well. Flavour with vanilla, pour over cherries and bake for 30 minutes in a moderately hot oven. Make meringue by whisking egg whites until stiff and fold in caster sugar. Pile on top of pie and return to oven for about 10 minutes for meringue to set and brown. Serve with cream.

Preserved Cherries: Make a strong sugar syrup by dissolving 12 oz. sugar in 1 pint water. Stone 2 lb. cherries, put them in the syrup, bring to the boil, remove and drain. Reduce syrup to ½ pint, pour it over the cherries, let them stand in it for some time, then spoon them out and lay them on a sieve to dry.

CURRANTS

Fresh Currant Layer Pudding: In a greased pudding basin, place a layer of stewed red or black currants, then a layer of suet pastry; repeat until basin is almost filled. Cover with greaseproof paper, and steam for 2 hours. When cooked turn out, cut into slices and serve with custard.

Blackcurrant Leaf Cream: Boil 1 lb. white sugar with ½ pint water and 8 tablespoons young blackcurrant leaves. Boil, without stirring, for 15 minutes; then strain and pour the hot syrup very gently on to 2 stiffly beaten egg whites. Beat all the time, until the mixture begins to thicken; then stir in the juice of a lemon and ¼ pint whipped cream. Serve in individual glasses.

DAMSONS

Baked Damsons: Pack the damsons closely into a pie dish sprinkle with sugar, and fill to just cover damsons with water. Cover closely and bake till the fruit is soft. Leave it covered till cold to prevent shrinkage. This method of cooking fruit in the oven rather than by stewing, was often used by country cooks when the oven was cooling down after the Sunday roast dinner. The amount of water added to the fruit was varied according to the water content of the fruit itself. Soft fruits such as raspberries require the addition of only one or two tablespoons of water as they make a lot of juice.

GOOSEBERRIES

Duck with Gooseberry Stuffing

I DUCK (ABOUT 5 LB.)	I TABLESPOON CHOPPED SAGE
SALT	SALT AND FRESHLY GROUND
8 OZ. GOOSEBERRIES	BLACK PEPPER
LIVER OF DUCK	5 OZ. SOFT BREADCRUMBS
I OZ. BUTTER	

Wash, dry and rub salt inside and outside of duck. Wash, top and tail gooseberries and chop 5 oz. finely. Fry liver in butter for 3 minutes, then mince or chop finely. Mix the sage, salt and pepper to taste into the breadcrumbs, stir in the liver and pan juices, and the chopped gooseberries. Stuff the duck with this mixture. Place on a trivet in a baking tin, and put into a moderately hot oven and cook for 2 hours, basting occasionally with fat from bird. Drain off surplus fat, and with a little fat, the stock from giblets and a little flour to thicken make a rich brown gravy. Strain and stir in 3 tablespoons sieved gooseberry purée made by cooking remaining gooseberries in a little water.

Gooseberry and Orange Pudding

I LB. GOOSEBERRIES	I ORANGE
SCANT ½ PINT WATER	I EGG
4 OZ. BROWN SUGAR	4 OZ. SOFT BREADCRUMBS
I OZ. BUTTER	

Simmer gooseberries in water with half the sugar. Cool. Melt the butter and grate in the orange rind, and squeeze in the juice. Beat gooseberries to a smooth pulp, add the beaten egg and tip in butter and orange mixture. Mix well. Butter a fireproof dish. Mix the rest of the sugar with the breadcrumbs and press round the sides and bottom of the dish. Keep back half for the top. Spoon in the gooseberry mixture without disturbing the crumb lining. Sprinkle the rest of the crumbs on top, cover with foil, and bake for 1 hour in a moderate oven. Remove foil for last 10 minutes to brown top. Good hot or cold with cream.

Gooseberry Salad: Arrange some lettuce leaves in a bowl. Arrange, in small mounds alternately on the leaves, about 8 oz.

diced, cooked potatoes, and a similar amount of diced, cooked beetroot. In the centre put 1 lb. of well drained gooseberries that have been cooked in water with a little sugar to taste. They should be tender but not broken. Use a little of the gooseberry syrup for sweetening a thick mayonnaise to pour over salad. Before serving, sprinkle with some chopped mint. Excellent served with cold lamb, or pork, or ham.

Gooseberry Tansy

1 QUART GOOSEBERRIES	8 OZ. FINE SOFT
3 OZ. BUTTER	BREADCRUMBS
4 EGGS	6 OZ. DEMERARA SUGAR

Cook gooseberries over gentle heat in the butter in close-lidded pan till soft. Sieve or beat into a pulp. Beat the eggs well and mix in the breadcrumbs and sugar. Blend this into the gooseberry pulp over a slow heat, stirring gently till the mixture is cooked firm. Do not allow to boil or mixture will curdle. Turn into a hot dish, sprinkle with sugar, and serve with hot cider or perry poured over. (This type of tansy is always made of soft fruit. It can be made with raspberries, mulberries or loganberries. Strawberries make a delicious tansy which can be topped with white wine for serving.)

Mixed Fruit

Red Fruit Compote: Take 1 lb. raspberries and 1 lb. black cherries, stoned. Put in a saucepan with just sufficient water to cover and bring slowly to the boil. Add sufficient sugar to sweeten and simmer for a few minutes, just until the fruit is soft but not mushy. Mix together 1 tablespoon cornflour with 2 tablespoons cold water and use to thicken the fruit. Bring back to the boil and simmer clear and no trace of cloudiness remains. Cool, pour into a glass serving dish and sprinkle the surface with split almonds. Serve very cold. Another method of making a summer fruit compote used to be popular with country housewives when there was a glut of soft fruit. Make a strong sugar syrup with 12 oz. sugar to 1 pint water and allow to cool slightly, dipping the fruit in a slotted draining spoon into the syrup to coat and piling up in a dish.

A Typical Fruit Cream

I LB. STRAWBERRIES	$\frac{1}{2}$ PINT DOUBLE CREAM,
SUGAR TO TASTE	WHIPPED OR $\frac{1}{4}$ PINT CREAM
2 TEASPOONS GELATINE	AND $\frac{1}{4}$ PINT CUSTARD
2–3 TABLESPOONS WATER OR	
FRUIT JUICE	

Sieve the fruit to make $\frac{1}{2}$ pint purée; add sugar. Dissolve the gelatine in the water or fruit juice in a basin over a pan of hot water. Pour into the purée stirring all the time. Fold in the cream (and custard if used). When the mixture is on the point of setting pour into a wetted mould or basin and leave to set. Raspberries, apricot purée, or $\frac{1}{2}$ pint fresh orange juice, or a mixture of raspberries and red currants may be used instead of strawberries, as well as blackberries and apple.

A Fruit Fool

I LB. GOOSEBERRIES	$\frac{1}{4}$ PINT DOUBLE CREAM,
SUGAR TO TASTE	WHIPPED
$\frac{1}{4}$ PINT CUSTARD	CHOPPED NUTS

Stew the fruit in a little water with sugar. Sieve the cooked fruit, or liquidise, fold the purée into the custard and cream. Pour into glasses and decorate with chopped nuts. Serve with sponge fingers. This can also be made with blackberries, raspberries, apricots, rhubarb, plums and damsons.

Summer Pudding

4 TABLESPOONS WATER
4 OZ. SUGAR
1½ LB. MIXED RED CURRANTS AND RASPBERRIES

6 OZ. WHITE BREAD, CUT IN THIN SLICES
WHIPPED CREAM OR CUSTARD

Mix the water and sugar and bring slowly to the boil. Add the fruit and stew gently until they are soft but retain their shape. Line a 1½-pint pudding basin with bread slices. Pour in the fruit and cover with more slices of bread. Place a saucer with a weight on it on top of the pudding and leave overnight in a cool place. Turn out and serve with whipped cream or custard. Other fruits such as black currants, damsons, blackberries and apple, may be used instead.

PEARS

Pear and Ginger Pudding

4 OZ. SOFT BREADCRUMBS
2 OZ. GRATED SUET
1 LB. COOKING PEARS
RIND 1 LEMON

SUGAR TO TASTE
1 OZ. CHOPPED, PRESERVED GINGER

Butter a pudding basin and coat with breadcrumbs. Mix remaining breadcrumbs with suet. Peel, core and grate pears mixing them with grated lemon rind, sugar to taste and the ginger. Put a third of bread mixture into the basin; then half the pears; cover with another third of bread mixture and remaining pears. Top with rest of bread mixture. Cover with greased paper and steam for 2 hours. Serve with a sweet sauce.

Pears in Red Wine: Peel cooking pears finely, leave them whole and with their stalks. Put them in a deep casserole with a liquor made from half red wine and half water, almost covering them. Add 6–8 oz. vanilla sugar according to amount of liquid (8 oz. for 1 pint), and cook in a slow oven for 3 hours, or, these can be left in oven all night at lowest marking. Pears will be tender and a deep red in colour. Serve in their own syrup, with cream.

Spiced Pears

4 FIRM, RIPE PEARS
3 OZ. CASTER SUGAR
½ PINT ORANGE JUICE
1 TABLESPOON LEMON JUICE
SMALL PINCH SALT

1 CINNAMON STICK, 2 INCHES
LONG
4 WHOLE CLOVES
⅛ TEASPOON GROUND NUTMEG

Peel, quarter and core pears. Place in a baking dish. Mix together sugar, juices, salt and spices and bring to the boil. Pour over pears. Cover and bake for 30 minutes in a moderate oven. Remove lid and cook for another 10 minutes or until pears are tender.

Coddled Pears in Rum Sauce

6 OZ. CASTER SUGAR
¼ PINT WATER
PINCH SALT
2 2-INCH CINNAMON STICKS
¼ TEASPOON WHOLE CLOVES

¼ TEASPOON WHOLE ALLSPICE
2 1-INCH GINGER ROOTS
6 FIRM, RIPE PEARS
⅛ PINT LIGHT RUM
6 SCOOPS LEMON WATER ICE

Mix sugar, water, salt and cinnamon. Tie cloves, allspice, ginger in a muslin bag and add. Bring to boil. Peel pears finely and leave whole with stems attached. Add to the syrup and cook slowly until pears are tender, 10–12 minutes, turning to cook uniformly. Remove spice bag. Add rum. Let pears stand in the syrup at least 24 hours. Just before serving, place a scoop of lemon ice in individual dishes. Stand a whole pear, stem up, on this. Spoon a little of the spiced rum sauce over the top.

PLUMS

Plum and Apple Savoury Sauce

1 LB. COOKING APPLES
8 OZ. PLUMS
1 OZ. BUTTER
PIECE OF LEMON PEEL

SALT AND PEPPER
PINCH THYME AND SAGE
 (DRIED)
SUGAR

Peel apples, core and quarter. Remove plum stones. Melt butter, add apples, plums and lemon peel, season with salt and pepper and mix in herbs. Cover and cook slowly until apples are soft. Remove lemon peel. Rub the fruit through a coarse sieve and return to a clean pan. Heat through, adding enough sugar to bring out the taste of the fruit without spoiling the tart, savoury flavour. Serve with a joint of meat.

Plum Caramel Pudding

BUTTER   DRY BREAD
SUGAR   RIPE PLUMS

Amounts of ingredients used will depend on size of dish, fruit available, etc. Coat the sides and bottom of a pie dish with butter. Sprinkle over with sugar. Line it neatly with slices of bread about ¼ inch thick. Place a layer of plums, cut in halves with stones removed, over the bread and sprinkle with sugar. Cover with a layer of bread and a second layer of plums and sugar. Finish the top with neat, even slices of bread and dabs of butter. Cover with a piece of greased paper and bake for an hour in a moderately hot oven. Serve with custard or cream. Greengages may be used.

Plums as Prunes: Place ripe plums close together, stalk ends uppermost, in a shallow wooden box. Cover with kitchen paper. Stand in a warm place for 24 hours. Afterwards, at every opportunity after the oven has been used and turned off, place the box of plums inside and leave the door open. As they shrink, re-arrange the plums closer together in the box. To speed up the final drying the box can be placed in a hot airing cupboard. When sufficiently dry, pack in airtight jars.

Note: This method is easy for the busy housewife with a large family who uses the oven every day. Otherwise, keep in a warm place during the day and put in the airing cupboard at night.

QUINCES

Quince Mould: Chop up 3 lb. quinces and simmer in enough water to cover with the juice and rind of 1 lemon, and leave overnight. Next day, add just enough dissolved gelatine to ensure a firm set (2 teaspoons per pint pulp dissolved in a little warm water). Rub the pulp through a sieve, reheat and sweeten to taste and, just before setting, stir in ¼ pint of whipped cream. Chill and turn out.

RASPBERRIES

Raspberry Flummery: The old recipe for a flummery was based on water in which oatmeal had been steeped overnight, boiled to a sort of syrupy gruel with sugar or honey and flavoured with orange-flower water or rose water. It was served with fruit and cream, especially with raspberries. Here is a modern version, which can hardly be called a flummery, but has much the same flavour.

Raspberry Chiffon: Gently stew 1 lb. raspberries and sweeten to taste. Melt a raspberry jelly in the strained juice, making up to 1 pint with water. Whisk up one small can of evaporated milk until trebled in volume (add 1 teaspoon of lemon juice if liked, to make it taste more like cream). Gradually whisk in the jelly, which should be quite cold and beginning to get syrupy. Pour over the raspberries in a glass bowl and allow to set.

RHUBARB

Pink Cream

2 LB. FORCED RHUBARB	RED FOOD COLOURING
6 OZ. CASTER SUGAR	$\frac{1}{3}$ PINT DOUBLE CREAM
3 TABLESPOONS WATER	$\frac{1}{2}$ TEASPOON VANILLA ESSENCE

Wash rhubarb and chop into pieces. Simmer with the sugar and water until soft. Whisk to a purée or put into an electric blender. Add a little colouring to make an attractive pink. Whip the cream with the vanilla added, fold into the rhubarb. Chill to serve.

Rhubarb in Spiced Batter

6 OZ. FLOUR	SUGAR
PINCH SALT	$\frac{1}{2}$ TEASPOON GROUND GINGER
2 EGGS	$\frac{1}{2}$ TEASPOON MIXED SPICE
MILK	$\frac{1}{2}$ TEASPOON COCOA
1 LB. RHUBARB	

Sieve the flour and salt into a bowl. Stir in the eggs and enough milk to make a batter, beat well and leave to stand. Wipe and cut rhubarb into small pieces. Arrange in a well-greased pie dish.

Sprinkle with sugar to taste. Beat the spices and cocoa into the batter. Pour over the rhubarb and bake in a hot oven until crisp.

Rhubarb and Mint Jelly: Choose rhubarb with pale pink stems. Wipe and cut into pieces. Stew with a little water until soft and pulpy, then strain through a fine sieve. To each pint of juice allow 1 lb. loaf sugar. Put juice and sugar into a preserving pan with some fresh, clean mint tied into bundles. Boil until jelly thickens when tested, stirring often. Remove mint before pouring into pots.

STRAWBERRIES

Strawberry Ice Cream

1 LB. STRAWBERRIES	3 EGG YOLKS
6 OZ. CASTER SUGAR	$\frac{1}{2}$ PINT SINGLE CREAM
$\frac{1}{4}$ PINT WATER	

Sieve or use a blender to reduce the strawberries to a purée. Add half the sugar and stir. Put the rest of the sugar and water in a saucepan, over a low heat. When sugar has dissolved, increase heat and boil for 5 minutes. Whisk the 3 egg yolks in a basin and gradually pour on hot syrup. Whisk well until mixture thickens. Now whisk in fruit purée and the cream. Stir all together and put into a freezing tray. Leave in freezing compartment of refrigerator for 2–3 hours, or until almost firm, then whisk again. Refreeze.

Household Uses

Flowers have always been used for beauty preparations, to provide dyes and cosmetics. So, to a lesser extent, have fruit juices, and some old remedies and tonics come from flowers.

Natural Rouge: Red flower petals, such as rose and geranium, can be crushed to obtain a harmless red dye to tint both lips and cheeks. Country girls always used these beauty aids, but during the Victorian era when cosmetics were taboo for ladies, they were used by most women.

Dandelion Root Dye: This particular hint is of gipsy origin, although most gardens contain dandelions, the most persistent of weeds. Soaked overnight in water, the root gives a bright magenta pink dye, the sort of colour gipsies love.

Dandelion Tea: Not worthy to be classed among the herbal teas, as the flavour is unpleasant, but it is a tonic, or was once believed so. Infuse 1 oz. of the flowers and leaves (not stalks) in a pint of boiling water for 10 minutes. Drink half a cupful before breakfast on three successive mornings; then, after a four-day pause, resume the dose for another three days. This treatment is said to clear the skin and brighten the eyes.

Dandelion Juice: The farmhouse cure for warts is to squeeze the milky juice from the stem on to the wart, and repeat the application several times a day until the wart withers.

Blackcurrant Dye: Milkmaids traditionally tinted their laces and ribbons in blackcurrant juice to dye them a delicate shade of mauve, and repeated soaking them in the juice several times.

Buttercup Ointment: Again, this is a gipsy cure, but most country dwellers find buttercups in the fields. Put 8 oz. pure vaseline into a pan with as many buttercup flower heads as can possibly be pressed into it. Allow to simmer without boiling for 45 minutes. While still hot, strain through muslin into small pots. When cold it is ready for use, and very good for skin troubles.

Marigold Ointment: Make as Buttercup Ointment. The flowers soaked in oil were used as a healing treatment for wounds, and have an excellent effect on old or badly healed scars. Marigold oil is also good to use for massaging tired feet. It can be applied to any kind of skin eruption (not allergic) or to small ulcers.

Strawberry Face-Pack: The beauties of Queen Anne's day used to give a mid-summer refresher to their complexions by blending

equal quantities of finely ground oatmeal, strawberry purée, and enough honey to make a smooth cream to spread over the face. When dry it was washed off with rose water.

Fresh Elderflower Water: A mild astringent and skin stimulant. Put about 8 oz. freshly picked elderflowers into a jar with one pint of boiling water. Cover closely, and set in a saucepan of boiling water to simmer gently for several hours. Strain through muslin. When cool, put into perfectly clean bottles that have been rinsed out with eau-de-cologne. Cork tightly. It will keep sweet for several weeks. If you add a wine glass of eau-de-cologne to each pint of elderflower water, it will keep much longer.

For Greasy Skins: After washing and drying the face, sponge with this lotion: 4 tablespoons elderflower water, $\frac{1}{2}$ teaspoon simple tincture of benzoin added drop by drop, stirring all the time; 5 drops tincture of myrrh (from the chemist).

Elderflower Cleansing Cream: Melt 1 lb. pure lard in a saucepan and add as many handfuls of elderflowers, stripped from stalks, as lard will cover. Simmer gently for about 1 hour. Strain through muslin. Add a few drops of oil of lavender or other good scent. Pour into pots and cover closely when cold. Use for the face.

Elderflower Hand Cream: Half-fill a screw-top jar with vaseline.

Add freshly gathered elderflowers, stripped from stalks, and pack them closely till the jar is quite full. Stand it to simmer in a pan of water, or cook gently in a slow oven, for some hours. The top should be put on lightly. While still hot, strain the mixture through muslin and bottle in jars. Excellent for rubbing into the hands after rough work.

Elderflower Ointment: Put 1 lb. white vaseline into a saucepan with as many elderflowers, without stems, as can possibly be pressed into it. Allow to simmer, not boil, for 45 minutes. While very hot, strain through muslin into small pots. It is ready for use when cold. Good for stings, chapped hands, and for nappy rash.

Green Elder Ointment: This was formerly popular as a household remedy for chilblains, sprains, bruises, etc. It was made from three parts fresh elder leaves, four parts of lard and two parts of suet. These ingredients were heated until all the colour was extracted, then strained under pressure through a cloth and allowed to cool.

Young Elder Leaves: Boiled in linseed oil they were used as a healing application to bruises and painful swellings. In 1659 it was written that water distilled in May from elder leaves, applied to a freckled face with a sponge 'at the wane of the moon', would remove freckles.

Elderberry Rob: From ancient times a 'Rob'—that is, a juice thickened by heat—has been made from elderberries and used as a cordial for coughs. Simmer 5 lb. fresh, crushed berries with 1 lb. loaf sugar and evaporate the juice to the thickness of honey. One or two tablespoons in a tumbler of hot water, taken at night, promotes perspiration and is soothing to the chest.

Sunflower Seed Cordial: Add 2 oz. sunflower seeds and a piece of green ginger to 2 pints of water. Simmer for an hour. Stir in 2 tablespoons clear honey. Strain and add 2 fluid oz. brandy. Bottle and seal to store. An invigorating tonic.

Sunflower Gin: Simmer 2 oz. sunflower seeds in 2 pints of water until the liquid is reduced to 1 pint. Strain, add sugar to taste, stirring to dissolve. Then mix in 6 fluid oz. gin. Bottle for storage.

Oil of Roses: Take 4 oz. sweet-smelling rosebuds (the white end cut away), bruise them well with a pestle, then put them in an earthenware pot. Pour 18 oz. olive oil over them and let them infuse for about a month in the sun or in a warm place, stirring them occasionally. Then bring the mixture to the boil, simmer for a few minutes. Pour the oil off, pressing and straining the flowers. Bottle when cool.

Violets, clove pinks or carnation, lavender, honeysuckle, etc., can be treated in the same way.

If the oil is not perfumed strongly enough, the last process can be repeated once or twice using fresh flowers, i.e. heated in the strained oil, pressing and straining them to release the fragrance.

Rose Water: This has been used since time immemorial for the beautifying of hands and face. Pink rose water is made by filling a saucepan with red rose petals, adding water to cover and bringing to the boil, allowing it to simmer for a few minutes. Allow to cool with lid still on the pan to retain the perfume, then strain and pour into glass bottles to be used when required. Select the most fragrant roses such as: Ena Harkness, Charles Mallerin, and Forty-Niner, with its fruity perfume. Not only do red roses possess the most powerful fragrance, but make rose water which is of a pleasing pink colour.

To Scent a Room: In Edward VI's time, 'having first burnt cypress wood to remove foul air, take 12 spoonfuls of bright red rose water, the weight of a sixpence in fine powder sugar, and boil it over hot embers. The room will smell as though it were full of roses.' (This optimistic advice was given in an old herbal book.)

Rose- or Scented-leaf Geranium: One of the smaller leaves in the bottom of a finger-bowl will give fragrance to the water. Line a cake tin with the scented leaves, and pour in a sponge mixture, then bake as usual. The lovely fragrance of the leaves imparts a delicious flavour to the sponge cake.

Lavender: This fragrant flower was introduced to England by the French Huguenots late in the sixteenth century, quickly became a favourite garden plant, and was taken to America by the Pilgrim Fathers. It was used for strewing, dried for use in sachets, and in pot-pourri. It was often used in perfumes still popular today.

Lavender Oil: Make as for oil of roses.

Lavender Water: Make as for rose water.

VEGETABLES

While primitive men were out hunting to provide meat for the cooking pot, women were engaged in the more gentle pursuit of gathering edible roots and leaves.

As far back as the Neolithic Age, it is thought that women started to plant a few vegetables, scratching in the soil near their caves with crude tools. Just as, in time, they learnt the value of herbs, they must have connected a sense of well-being with eating certain vegetables. So these were the ones which were sought out to fill the pot, and an effort was made to grow more of them.

By the late Bronze Age, when the first plough replaced the hoe in agriculture, it was possible to grow crops of all kinds on a larger scale. But Ancient Britons apparently were content with the many wild varieties which were abundant here—kale, a stalky kind of cabbage, thin strong-flavoured leeks, and near the coast a kind of wild sea beet. It was more a question of transplanting vegetables to a convenient place where they could be easily gathered, than attempting to improve the strain, or develop new species.

Outside Britain, early civilisations were growing a wide range of vegetables. Cabbage, asparagus, peas, beans, seakale and onions were known to the Greeks. The Romans enjoyed peas, beans, turnips, carrots, parsnips, beet, radish, sorrel, asparagus, onions, garlic, cucumbers, chicory, lettuce, parsley, mustard, mushrooms —as well as many herbs. Before the Romans came here, the vegetables grown in Britain were mainly developments of those mentioned above, and a type of asparagus, all of which grew wild. Other wild plants good to eat, chicory and celery, were no doubt neglected because no one had yet discovered that they could be made more edible by blanching the stems. The Romans, however, are generally given credit not only for planting our orchards and herb gardens, but for considerably extending the range of our vegetables. Unfortunately these followed the same sad pattern, after the Romans left, as the herbs, flowers and fruit they introduced. Many naturalised, some disappeared altogether. Others vanished from the British table, only to re-appear as newcomers in an improved form, centuries later.

The leek garden

Early Saxon records show that leeks were tremendously popular, so much so that the vegetable patch was coming to be called the leek garden, and the gardener the 'leekward'. There were also a number of other roots and plants in it which have since lost favour. For instance, in our time 'potherbs' mean carrots, turnips and onions, and one often hears older women at country markets ask for a pound of potherbs for a stew. But throughout the Middle Ages our ancestors flavoured their soups and broths with alexanders—called the black potherb, from the darkness of its colour —and the corn salad, or white potherb. Both herbs are found wild today in many parts of Britain, the black potherb being particularly plentiful on the south-west of the Isle of Anglesey. Its health-giving properties were well recognised by seafaring men, and stories used to be told of crews being allowed to go ashore at Anglesey, especially to gather and cook the herb. The white potherb seems to have been eaten generally as a salad. The introduction of more succulent root vegetables, and of blanched celery, into general use, made the old potherbs superfluous, and they gradually reverted to their original wild state.

It is interesting to look at the vegetables we now take for granted, note when they first arrived in Britain, and realise the limited variety that existed before the sixteenth century.

Beans, Scarlet Runners: Introduced into England from South America in 1633, the plant was treated solely as an ornamental climber until some time in the eighteenth century when it was discovered that the pods were edible.

Beetroot: Stems from the wild sea beet growing on British sea shores, but was not cultivated until 1546.

Broccoli: One of the branches of sea cabbage, still growing wild here, developed and improved in Italy, introduced here in the seventeenth century.

Brussels Sprouts: Another of the descendants from sea cabbage. Known and eaten by the Belgians since the thirteenth century, but not grown in England on any scale until the nineteenth century.

Cabbage: Originated from a wild cabbage variety which grows on the shores of the Mediterranean as well as southern England.

Carrot: This is the most recent of all root vegetables to be used as human food. It was developed from a wild plant which was poisonous. French and German plant breeders eliminated the poison and gave us the field carrot for cattle in the days of Elizabeth I. The garden carrot for human consumption was a much later development.

Cauliflower: A member of the cabbage family, developed in Southern Europe, and has been grown in Britain only since the seventeenth century.

Celery: Wild celery or 'smallage' is common in ditches and marshy places in lowlands all over the world. Garden celery as we know it was developed in Italy, and became accepted as a vegetable in Britain early in the nineteenth century.

Cucumber: The progenitor of the cultivated cucumber came from India, and from there it travelled to Egypt, then later via the Romans to Britain.

Kale: Comes nearest to the original wild cabbage. Its name comes from the Latin *caulis* meaning a stalk, and the early wild British cabbages were probably more stalk than anything else.

Leek: This vegetable is perhaps the oldest recorded in British history, and still grows wild in many places.

Lettuce: Some wild species always grew in Britain, but the cultivated type eaten in salads was introduced by the Romans. 'Sallets' made of lettuce became popular in Elizabethan times.

Onion: The common garden onion is a native of Western Asia, and was grown by the Egyptians. It is not certain, but, as the name we use comes from the Latin, it is assumed the Romans brought it here.

Parsnips: A native root that was cultivated long before the introduction of the potato, and used to be eaten with meat, much as the potato is eaten now.

Potato: Came from South America. Was first imported into Britain in mid-sixteenth century, and then a more popular variety introduced in the nineteenth century.

Radish: There is a wild radish occurring as a weed in Britain, but the garden radish is considered to be the oriental species, which came from Southern Asia some time in the mid-sixteenth century.

Shallot: Is a native of Palestine, and was brought back to this country by the returning Crusaders in medieval times.

Spinach: Originated in the Far East, and was introduced to Britain about the mid-sixteenth century.

Swede: A hybrid developed from the turnip and some other member of the cabbage family. First grown in Sweden in 1781, introduced here shortly afterwards.

Tomato: Originated in South America. It came to Britain in the sixteenth century, when it was called the love apple, but until the nineteenth century was grown for decoration only.

Turnip: Probably originated from the wild turnip in Europe, grown from very ancient times, but first cultivated for the table in England in 1650.

A garden was an essential part of all monastic institutions and vegetables were extensively grown in them. Every manor and most farms possessed gardens and orchards, many of them very large. London, easily the largest and most important city of the Middle Ages, had probably the first true market gardens. For many years before 1345 the gardeners of the nobility sold surplus produce near the gate of St. Paul's churchyard, but by that year the market had grown to such an extent that it hindered the traffic 'both on foot and on horseback'. Eventually the market found a home outside the city walls in what had once been a convent garden—Covent Garden today—from which it is shortly to be moved again.

The practice of growing vegetables, not only in the gardens of wealthy landowners but also in the small plots of the cottages and farms developed rapidly during the sixteenth century. And, as the garden was regarded as an adjunct of the kitchen and the still-room, it was considered a woman's province. Barnaby Googe, a contemporary writer, records: 'Herein were the olde husbands very careful and used always to judge that where they found the Garden out of order, the wife of the house (for unto her belonged the charge whereof) was no good huswyfe.'

By the time of Henry VIII a much wider range of fruit and vegetables, both homegrown and from the Continent, had become available. Melons, pumpkins and gourds of all kinds began to appear, and there were plenty of the traditional leeks, onions and garlic. Globe artichokes were now mentioned frequently—their chief use seems to have been for boiling in beef broth. A cauliflower is pictured in Gerard's *Herball*, but it does not seem to have been common.

Vegetables and the Elizabethans

At the beginning of the reign of Queen Elizabeth, British horti-culture received a fillip from an influx of Protestant refugees from the Continent, a number of whom brought that skill in intensive market gardening for which the Dutch, Walloons and French have been famous for many years. The coast towns of Kent, Essex and Suffolk received the main stream of these refugees. Finding suitable soil around Sandwich, some of them began to develop vegetable growing and very soon, according to Samuel Smiles writing in *The Huguenots*: 'the cabbage, carrots and celery produced by the foreigners met with so ready a sale and were so much in demand in London itself, that a body of gardeners shortly afterwards removed from Sandwich and settled at Wands-worth, Battersea and Bermondsey where many of the rich garden-grounds first planted by the Flemings, still continue to be the most productive in the neighbourhood of the metropolis'.

It was during Elizabeth's reign that the first potatoes were brought to England from the 'coast of Guinea and the Indies of Nova Hispania' by Sir John Hawkins in 1564, but it was about a hundred years later that the potato came into its own as a cheap form of food, and they were then being imported from Ireland where they had been introduced by Sir Walter Raleigh when he was governor there. The story goes that he first decided to sample them himself, and his cook boiled up the leaves for him. As it is one of those plants of which one part is poison while the rest is wholesome food, Sir Walter was so ill that he ordered all the potatoes to be destroyed. Fortunately, a few were saved, and someone recollected that it was the tubers, not the leaves that should be eaten. And thus potatoes came to be grown in Ireland.

Tomatoes were known as far back as 1544, when they had come to Europe by way of Mexico. But these early tomatoes were ribbed, rather ugly fruit, which were grown more as a curiosity and regarded in Britain as unfit for eating, though known to be enjoyed by Spaniards and other foreigners. It was not until the nineteenth century, that a mutation occurred which brought the smooth, round tomato and on this an industry began to build up.

As the population in Britain grew, so the cultivation of produce for human consumption increased with it. Many new species and varieties coming in from foreign countries were being propagated and sold by the nurserymen. During the eighteenth century nurseries selling plants and trees became numerous. Carrots became more popular, potatoes flourished. Salsify and celery also came into prominence.

But it was not until the middle of the nineteenth century that market gardening and fruit-growing became a major industry. Vegetables and fruit were improved by selective breeding and culture, though few new plants other than the tomato were introduced for commercial use. The cauliflower trade started around 1836. About 1860 glasshouses became more widely used, while smaller growers started to use cloches and frames.

Grow your own vegetables

All this so-called 'intensive' culture of vegetables was still a far cry from the methods employed today: fertilisers to get the most from the soil, insecticides and pesticides to avoid losses. Some of the old vegetables which were highly prized, did not compare well in appearance with the regular-shaped, even-sized and brightly coloured modern equivalents. But it is generally accepted that they had more flavour, and did not carry the side-effects of chemical sprays. Perhaps the resurgence of interest in compost-grown vegetables is an historical necessity. But apart from the health aspect, freshly picked vegetables taste quite unlike those that have travelled to market, thence to the shop, and often pre-packaged before they are bought for cooking.

E

Home-grown vegetables are the answer, if you have space in your garden. They will be uncontaminated, cost less after your initial outlay, and can look attractive while growing. A row of Scarlet Runners with their bright red flowers is a delight to the eye, and many vegetables when they flower are surprisingly pretty: the golden trumpet flowers of the marrows and cucumbers with their vine-like leaves, salsify with its exotic bluish-purple flower, even the mauve flower of the sprouting broccoli.

Then, not to be despised, is the great excitement to be had from vegetable growing. It can be almost unbelievable how many beans come from one bean plant; the fat carrots you can have from half a teaspoon of seeds; the marrow that suddenly appears and seems to swell overnight after the flowerhead has fallen; the trusses of green tomatoes changing colour as they ripen, and a line of kohlrabi looking like plants from another planet.

You will then be able to try out many of the recipes given in this book. From the rather odd wording, you will appreciate that some of them are very old indeed, but that is part of their charm and I would not have changed them for the world.

Artichokes (Jerusalem): Simmer gently until tender in just sufficient water to cover, with a little salt and a teaspoon of lemon juice or vinegar to keep them white.

Smothered Artichokes: Melt 2 oz. butter in a heavy saucepan, turn about 12 peeled and halved large artichokes in this until well coated. Add 2 leeks, cleaned and chopped into ½-inch lengths, stir gently and just cover with chicken stock. Put the lid on the pan and simmer until the artichokes are just tender. (Add about a

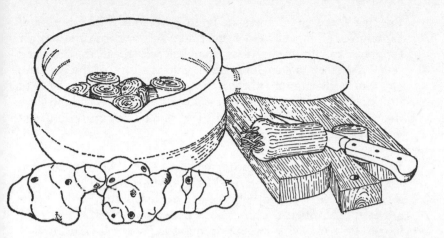

teaspoon of lemon juice or vinegar, if liked, to keep vegetables white.) Moisten 1 tablespoon cornflour with 2 tablespoons milk, stir in ¼ pint milk and water mixed, pour into the saucepan. Cook over low heat, stirring gently until the sauce becomes thick and smooth, season to taste with salt and pepper.

Artichokes with Bacon: Parboil finely peeled artichokes in well salted water with a squeeze of lemon juice. Render out the fat from 2 chopped rashers of streaky bacon, add well drained artichokes to the pan and turn gently to coat in the fat. Serve hot.

Asparagus: Try to cook in bundles of even length and thickness, standing upright in a deep saucepan so that the woody ends are in the boiling water, and the tips are merely steamed. Cover the pan and simmer until tender. Add very little salt to the water.

Asparagus Soup

1 SMALL BUNDLE ASPARAGUS	3 TABLESPOONS FLOUR
1 SMALL ONION, FINELY SLICED	SALT AND PEPPER
1 PINT WHITE STOCK	½ PINT MILK
2 OZ. BUTTER	2–3 TABLESPOONS CREAM

Wash asparagus, trim and discard woody part of stem, and cut remainder into short lengths, keeping a few tips for garnish. Cook the tips for 5–10 minutes in boiling salted water. Put rest of asparagus, onion, ¼ pint stock and butter in a saucepan and simmer for about 20 minutes, until asparagus is soft. Blend the flour and remaining stock to a smooth cream. Stir in a little of the hot soup and return this mixture to the pan; bring to the boil, stirring until it thickens. Cook for further 2–3 minutes. Season to taste and sieve the soup, or liquidise it. Stir in the milk and cream, re-heat and garnish with the asparagus tips.

Broad Beans: The first picking of beans should be so young and tender that they can be cooked in a few minutes in fast boiling salted water and served with a little melted butter. Older beans are easily identified because the scar becomes black. They need longer, slower cooking and may require to be sieved. The purée is delicious masked with a little parsley sauce or savoury white sauce with roughly chopped hard-boiled egg in it. Cold cooked left-over beans can be served, if young and tender, as a salad to accompany cold meats, in a vinaigrette sauce.

Green Beans (Scarlet Runners or French Beans): Remove tips and strings if necessary, leave whole, or cut into 1-inch pieces, or slice lengthwise. Place 1 lb. prepared beans in a saucepan with about 1 inch boiling salted water. Cook uncovered for about 5 minutes. Cover and cook 10–12 minutes or until beans are just tender. Cook whole beans 2–3 minutes longer. Drain if necessary and add salt and black pepper to taste. Toss lightly in 1 oz. butter, margarine or bacon fat.

Green Beans with Nutmeg Butter: Cook 1 lb. fresh beans, as above, then melt 1½ oz. butter or margarine, add ¼ teaspoon nutmeg, ⅛ teaspoon ground black pepper. Pour over cooked beans. Mix lightly. Serve hot.

Beetroot: Needs to be handled carefully as it bleeds easily. Wash the beet and boil till tender. Leave to become cool in the water in which it was boiled. Wipe off the skins, trim and slice into vinegar, and serve at once.

Baked Beet: Choose even sized beets and cook as above. Skin, then pile round the joint in the roasting tin. Pour over a little of the dripping from the joint, sprinkle well with nutmeg, and serve, after baking in oven 20–25 minutes with joint, piping hot. They bring out the flavour of roast pork or beef.

Beetroot with Marjoram: Boil about 2 lb. fresh beetroot until tender. Melt 1½ oz. butter, blend in 2 teaspoons fresh lemon juice, ½ teaspoon salt, ⅛ teaspoon ground black pepper, ½ teaspoon dried or 1 teaspoon chopped marjoram. Peel and slice beets. Add lemon butter and mix lightly. Serve garnished with crisp fried onion rings.

Beetroot Soup: Scrub clean about 1 lb. beetroots and grate them raw into ½ pint good beef stock. Add ½ teaspoon salt, 1 teaspoon sugar, 1 teaspoon lemon juice. Cover and cook for 15 minutes until beets are tender. Put through a coarse sieve. Add another ¾ pint stock and ½ teaspoon fennel seed. Heat. Serve hot, each serving topped with a tablespoon sour cream and a sprinkling of chopped parsley.

Broccoli: As well as the usual boiling method, it can be tied in bunches and cooked standing upright in the bottom part of a double boiler, containing about 2 inches boiling water and 1 teaspoon salt. Cover with lid and cook 15–20 minutes. Serve with melted butter, vinaigrette or white sauce.

Broccoli with Egg Sauce: Wash and trim off tough portion of stems of 1½ lb. broccoli. Boil in about ½ pint chicken stock for 15 minutes or until just tender, lifting cover occasionally to keep bright green colour. Drain. Place on toast. Have ready ¾ pint white sauce combined with a chopped hard-boiled egg. Spoon over the broccoli. Slice another hard-boiled egg and place a slice on each serving.

Brussels Sprouts: To keep them green trim well and drop them into fast boiling salted water, cook very rapidly, drain thoroughly, and serve hot.

Sprouts with Herbs: Cook about 1½ lb. sprouts as directed. Drain and cover with sauce. Melt 2 oz. butter or margarine, blend in 1 oz. flour. Remove from heat and gradually stir in ¾ pint milk.

Add ½ teaspoon salt, ⅛ teaspoon black pepper, ½ teaspoon chopped marjoram, ½ teaspoon chopped thyme. Return to heat, and cook, stirring, until thick. Garnish sauce-covered sprouts with parsley.

Sprouts with Chestnuts: Boil ½ lb. chestnuts for 15 minutes, and peel. Prepare and cook the sprouts, as directed above, with the peeled chestnuts. Drain, add butter, pepper and salt to taste.

Sprouts with Almonds: Heat and drain a small can of water chestnuts, slice and mix with the cooked sprouts together with 2 oz. flaked almonds, lightly browned in 1 oz. butter. Season to taste with salt and pepper.

Cabbage: Cook quickly in a covered pan with as little water as possible to retain the crisp texture and fresh green colour. Add a knob of butter to the pan to give the cabbage a nice gloss, and shake from time to time while it is cooking to prevent it from sticking to the bottom. Allow 12–15 minutes. The flavour of a white drumhead cabbage is improved by the addition of 1 or 2 teaspoons of caraway seeds. Drain well before serving and season.

Curried Cabbage: Shred cabbage very finely. Toss about 1 lb. shredded cabbage in 1 oz. melted butter over a moderate heat, until it goes limp. Sprinkle with ½ teaspoon curry powder and ½ teaspoon turmeric. Add salt to taste and stir cabbage until seasoning is well distributed. This dish can be finished in various ways, by stirring in 2 tablespoons of fresh single cream, or sour cream. Cream cheese can also be added which melts as it is combined with the hot cabbage.

Cabbage Salad: Use chopped celery, apple, grated carrot, horseradish and any other crisp vegetable to mix with finely chopped cabbage. Softer vegetable ingredients become messy. Mix with a vinaigrette sauce or mayonnaise.

Hot Cole Slaw: Shred a medium-sized cabbage and immerse in boiling water for 1 minute. Drain well. Remove to serving bowl. Combine 2 teaspoons salt, ¼ teaspoon ground black pepper, 1 teaspoon dill seed, ½ teaspoon sugar, ¼ pint sour cream and 2 tablespoons wine vinegar. Add to cabbage. Toss and serve.

Thin-end Cabbage: This way of cooking white or red cabbage is so called in Sussex because it makes quite a substantial dish out of a vegetable at the time countryfolk call the thin end of the year. Remove the hard stalk from the cabbage, cut it in quarters, or eighths if a large one. Fast boil in salted water until just tender, strain off the water and reserve ½ pint. Stir 2 oz. butter or dripping into the cooked cabbage, then sprinkle on and stir in 1 tablespoon flour. Add 1 teaspoon sugar and 1 tablespoon malt tarragon vinegar. Gradually add sufficient of the water to make a slightly thickened sauce. Cook for a further 3–4 minutes, stirring gently. Serve with boiled bacon, or hand of pork.

Red Cabbage Salad: Shred a red cabbage and an onion very finely. Pour over a dressing made with 1 tablespoon honey, 2 tablespoons vinegar, ½ teaspoon ground black pepper well mixed. Serve with cold meat.

Carrots: It is worth the trouble to cook even the first thinnings from a row of carrots as they have a delicious nutty flavour. Wash and trim them well, boil for a few minutes only in lightly salted water, drain and serve tossed in butter. Larger carrots can be cooked in the same way, sliced into rings, and seasoned with a little nutmeg as well as salt and pepper. Another way is to drain the cooked carrots, add ½ oz. butter and 2 teaspoons of soft brown sugar, and shake over moderate heat until the butter and sugar melt together. I prefer carrots cooked this way with a little grated orange zest added to them, at the same time as the butter and sugar.

Carrot Pie

8 OZ. SHORTCRUST PASTRY	½ TEASPOON GROUND NUTMEG
8 OZ. SUGAR	⅛ TEASPOON GROUND CLOVES
1 TABLESPOON FLOUR	3 EGGS
½ TEASPOON SALT	12 OZ. MASHED COOKED
1 TEASPOON GROUND GINGER	CARROTS
1 TEASPOON GROUND CINNAMON	½ PINT SINGLE CREAM OR
⅛ TEASPOON GROUND BLACK	EVAPORATED MILK
PEPPER	

Line a 9-inch pie dish with the pastry. Mix together the sugar, flour, salt and spices. Beat in the eggs. Stir in the carrots and cream. Pour into the pastry-lined dish. Bake in a preheated oven, moderately hot, for 50 minutes or until a knife inserted in the centre comes out clean. Cool.

Curried Carrots: Combine 1 lb. coarsely grated carrots, 6 oz. firm, fresh pineapple wedges, 3 tablespoons soft brown sugar, 1½ oz. butter or margarine, 3 tablespoons hot water, ¼ teaspoon salt (or to taste), 1 teaspoon curry powder. Cover saucepan and cook about 7 minutes or until pineapple and carrot are tender. Serve hot with pork or poultry.

Cauliflower: Trim off any coarse outer leaves, make a cross cut in the base of the stem and rinse well under cold running water. Cook, stalk down, in gently boiling salted water so that the head comes above the level of the water and is steamed. Drain well.

Cauliflower au Gratin: Make a thick savoury sauce with 1 oz. butter, 1 oz. flour, ¼ pint milk and sufficient water from the cooked cauliflower to give a good coating consistency. Season to taste with pepper, salt and made mustard. Pull pan aside from heat and stir in 2–4 oz. grated strong Cheddar cheese. When the cheese has melted, put the drained cauliflower in a fireproof serving dish, pour the sauce over, sprinkle a few browned bread-crumbs on top and finish under a hot grill.

Cauliflower Cream Soup: Trim and clean a large cauliflower, cook gently in 2 pints salted water until tender, press through a sieve or liquidise. To keep white, add 2 teaspoons lemon juice if liked. Cook together 1 oz. butter and 1 oz. flour with ½ pint milk to make a sauce, season with nutmeg, salt and pepper, stir in the cauliflower purée and ¼ pint cream.

Cauliflower Pickle: Tender white florets are attractive in a mixed pickle. In some parts of the country the sprigs are arranged in alternate layers with chunks of cucumber and onions to make traditional patterns, showing through the sides of the glass jar.

Cauliflower Salads: The sprigs can be chopped and mixed with chopped celery and apple combined with a little salad cream. Or boil little sprigs for a few minutes until just tender. Drain and toss them in a vinaigrette sauce (2 parts of oil, 1 of vinegar), and garnish with chopped parsley or chives.

Celery: To serve raw wash in cold running water, quarter and stand upright in a celery jug. Crisp, appetising and tasty it is also good for rheumatism. To braise, put the well-cleaned and trimmed celery heads in a saucepan with just enough water to cover and 1–2 teaspoons Marmite, cover and simmer until tender.

Celery Boats: Medium thick celery stalks, cut into 3-inch pieces and filled with various savoury mixtures make a nice supper dish. In some country pubs it was the custom to serve the celery hearts with the traditional ploughman's lunch of bread and cheese and use the outer stalks filled in this way as an attraction for evening customers. Fill with cream cheese and chopped walnuts or shallots.

Braised Celery in Cider: Butter a shallow baking dish well and pack with nicely washed and trimmed celery sticks. Cover with dry cider, sprinkle with salt and pepper and dot with more butter. Cover and bake for 25—30 minutes in a moderate oven. Serve hot.

Boiled Celery: Keep the rinds and trimmings of bacon and add to the water in which the celery is boiled. Add no salt and only just sufficient water to cover the celery. Drain cooked celery well and serve sprinkled with chopped parsley.

E*

Celery and Apple Hot Pot: Peel and core 2 large cooking apples. Grease a deep pie dish, place a thin slice of gammon in the bottom, cover with a layer of sliced apple, then a layer of onion, very thinly sliced. Chop up the outer stalks from a large head of celery, wash well and add to the pie dish. Cover with more sliced apple and onion, finishing with another slice of gammon, cut in strips. Pour over ¼ pint well-seasoned white stock and bake in a moderately hot oven for 40–45 minutes, covering the top with foil if it becomes too brown before the vegetables are cooked.

Courgettes: These tiny marrows or zucchini are now popular and can be grown in this country. Wash them before using, but do not peel. They taste good sliced and sweated in a little butter with a finely chopped onion and chopped tomatoes.

Cucumber: To eliminate the slightly bitter flavour of a large cucumber, peel and slice thinly, and spread out the slices on a board. Sprinkle generously with salt, leave to stand for about 20 minutes and rinse off the salty liquid with cold running water through a colander. Serve in salads.

Cucumber Cups: This is a good way to use up a cucumber which has become rather coarse, so that the seeds require to be removed. Peel the cucumber and cut into 3-inch chunks. Scoop out the seeds and cook the thick rings gently in a little white stock until tender but not mushy. Drain well. stand upright on rounds of crisply fried bread and fill centres with cooked green peas.

Simmered Cucumbers: Peel 2 medium-sized cucumbers and slice into ¼-inch slices. Put into 4 tablespoons boiling water with ½ teaspoon salt. Cover and simmer until tender, 7–10 minutes. Add 2 teaspoons butter and sprinkle with a tablespoon chopped parsley, chives or mint.

Cucumber with Yogurt and Mint: Wash and slice finely a good-sized cucumber. Add to a carton of yogurt, a teaspoon bruised, chopped mint, salt and pepper to taste. Mix in the cucumber. Makes a salad or side dish with curry.

Horse-radish: Unlike other root vegetables commonly grown in the kitchen garden, this is extremely strongly flavoured and can only be used in small quantities as a seasoning.

Creamed Horse-radish: Whip ¼ pint double cream until fairly stiff. Fold in 1 tablespoon strong horse-radish sauce and a little made mustard to give the sauce a good colour.

Horse-radish and Apple Sauce: Peel, core and slice 1 large cooking apple. Cook with very little water to a fluffy purée. Beat in freshly grated horse-radish to taste, according to the strength preferred, and colour pink with a little vinegar from a dish of cooked beetroot. If liked, dice some of the beetroot and add to the sauce, which can be served hot with all kinds of fish or cold with roast pork instead of the usual apple sauce.

Horse-radish Vinegar: This old recipe comes from a farmhouse kitchen where the cooking range rarely went out. Once hot, the covered containers could be put in an airing cupboard or any really warm place to infuse. Peel and slice up a small onion, or a shallot. Put it into a stone jar and pour over 1 pint of warm cider vinegar. Stand at the back of the stove or in a warm place. Add as much shredded horse-radish as the jar will hold, cover it tightly and leave for 1 hour. Open, press down the horse-radish and add more to fill the jar. Infuse, covered, for several days. Strain vinegar, bring to boil and bottle while still hot.

Kale: A winter standby that can be cooked like spinach.

Kale with Marjoram: Wash 2 lb. kale and cut off tough stems. Place in a saucepan with 2 tablespoons chopped onion, ¾ teaspoon salt, 1 teaspoon chopped marjoram, ½ teaspoon sugar, ⅛ teaspoon ground black pepper. Cover and cook for 20 minutes or until tender. Add 1 oz. bacon fat, mix well, and serve.

Leeks: They need little water in cooking. Clean them carefully and lay flat in a shallow, well-buttered dish. Pour on a little milk or stock, a knob of butter and seasoning to taste. Cover closely and cook in a moderate oven until tender. Or cut in rings, then cook very quickly in a covered pan in a little seasoned butter.

Cock-a-Leekie

3–4 LB. BOILING FOWL
2 OZ. BUTTER OR MARGARINE
3 PINTS WATER
SALT TO TASTE
12 OZ. FINELY CHOPPED LEEKS
1 MEDIUM CARROT, FINELY DICED
5 STALKS CELERY, FINELY DICED

5 TABLESPOONS CHOPPED
  PARSLEY
1 TEASPOON CHOPPED THYME
$\frac{1}{4}$ TEASPOON GROUND BLACK
  PEPPER
$\frac{1}{4}$ TEASPOON GARLIC POWDER
1$\frac{1}{2}$ OZ. PEARL BARLEY

Joint the fowl, wash, and wipe dry. Fry on all sides over gentle heat in butter. Add water and salt. Cover and simmer for 1$\frac{1}{2}$–2 hours or until meat falls from the bones. Lift fowl from pot and remove from bones. Skim excess fat from stock. Return meat together with remaining ingredients. Cover and cook about 20 minutes until vegetables are tender. Serve hot.

Leeks Vinaigrette: Using only the white part of the leeks, cut into equal lengths. Cook for 10–15 minutes in salted water. Drain and dress with vinaigrette sauce (2 parts of oil, 1 of vinegar). Garnish with chopped parsley.

Lettuce: Used mainly in salads, it is good to know that it can be cooked as well, especially should you be faced with a row of bolting lettuce that needs picking. It can be cooked in very little water, as spinach, served well seasoned and with a good knob of butter. It also makes a good dish cooked with young peas, taking no longer than the peas to cook.

Jonquil Salad: Rinse some cabbage lettuce, drain and dry thoroughly. Break into convenient pieces. Have ready 3 hard-boiled eggs. Rub the salad bowl with a clove of garlic or, if preferred, a spring onion. Arrange a layer of lettuce, then a few slices of egg. Repeat until the bowl is full. Put 2 tablespoons sugar in a bowl, add a pinch of salt, ¼ teaspoon mustard. Blend with ¼ pint cream. Then beat in, very carefully, sufficient white vinegar to make the dressing thick. Pour over salad and serve immediately.

Lettuce Soup

1½ PINTS SHELLED PEAS	2 TEASPOONS SUGAR
1 LARGE LETTUCE HEART	SALT TO TASTE
3 OZ. BUTTER	2 PINTS WATER

Put the peas and the lettuce heart which has been washed and shredded, in a saucepan with the melted butter. Add sugar and salt. Cook very slowly for 10–12 minutes, shaking now and again so that all is thoroughly mixed with the melted butter. Now add the water, and cook until peas are tender. Sieve, return to pan, season to taste, re-heat.

Marrow: Young marrows can be peeled, cut in slices and the pith removed, then steamed in a colander over boiling water. Sprinkle with salt and pepper and dot with butter just before serving as soon as the rings begin to turn transparent. Older marrows are better used for stuffing and if slightly woody should be blanched in boiling water before stuffing and baking in the oven.

Stuffed Marrow: Peel, slice in half lengthwise and scoop out the seeds. Fill with a stuffing which includes a little suet, chopped fat bacon or butter to keep it moist. Mound up the stuffing well in the centre, put the lid in place and secure with thread which can easily be cut and removed after the marrow is cooked, or wooden cocktail sticks. Bake in a moderately hot oven, basting with melted butter frequently for 1 hour or until marrow is tender.

Fillings: Minced left-over cooked lamb, mixed with thick brown gravy, chopped tomatoes, salt and pepper and chopped parsley can be bound with an egg. Baked beans mixed with chopped fat bacon, a little grated cheese and fresh white breadcrumbs, are also good.

Macedoine with Marrow: The usual selection of mixed fresh young vegetables, lightly cooked and diced, can be varied by the addition of marrow. Try dicing the flesh of a young marrow, steam it and mix with sliced cooked carrots and peas. Toss all in butter and serve well seasoned with salt, pepper and nutmeg.

Marrow and Rhubarb Chutney: Rhubarb begins to get rather coarse in the garden at the same time as you may have a glut of marrows. Peel and cut up a large marrow, removing the pith, into cubes. Add sufficient thick stalks of rhubarb, also cubed, to make about $2\frac{1}{2}$ lb. in weight. Put in a bowl, sprinkling salt between the layers, leave overnight. Put a peeled and chopped onion, $\frac{1}{2}$ oz. salt, 4 oz. each sultanas, currants and brown sugar into a large saucepan. Season with 1 teaspoon each ground ginger and mustard seed, add $\frac{1}{2}$ pint vinegar, bring to the boil, add the drained marrow and rhubarb, simmer until cooked, about $1\frac{1}{2}$ hours. Pour into clean hot jars and seal at once. Store for several months before using to improve the flavour.

Mixed Vegetables: A mixture of diced, cooked root vegetables and cooked peas or chopped French beans makes a delicious hot macedoine, or when cold, add mayonnaise to make Russian salad.

White Winter Soup: Melt 1 oz. butter and add 2 sticks of celery, 2 leeks and 2 onions all well chopped. Cook gently for 10 minutes, stirring to prevent sticking. Pour on $1\frac{1}{2}$ pints white stock, season and simmer till vegetables are soft. Pass through a sieve, return to the saucepan and add milk. Re-heat, and serve with croûtons or chopped chives or parsley.

White Winter Salad: Peel, core, quarter and slice an apple, sprinkle it with lemon juice to retain its colour. Mix this with about 1 lb. finely chopped white cabbage, grated celeriac (or root ends of celery), a small finely chopped onion, a tablespoon of hazel nuts. Season to taste and dress with salad cream, or a mixture of sour cream and lemon juice. Serve surrounded with slices of tomato or beetroot.

Summer Soup: Slice, cube or cut into small shapes about ½ pint mixed vegetables (green beans, peas, asparagus, young carrots etc.). Cook in salted water until soft, then drain. Bring 2 pints clear stock to the boil, add vegetables, season, and serve very hot.

Nettles: When young, they can be cooked in the same way as spinach but the stems must be discarded as these are tough and woody. Wear old gloves and gather a large quantity as, like spinach, they cook down considerably. Wash in several waters, and press down in a large pan under a weight, adding more nettles after a few minutes. There should be sufficient water left from rinsing to cook the nettles without burning. Cover and cook until soft, stirring occasionally, for about 15 minutes. Drain well.

Onions: As these form part of so many dishes, it is important to remember that some varieties are much more strongly flavoured than others. The large Spanish onions are quite mild, and shallots have a very delicate flavour indeed, making them suitable for use raw sliced or grated. Spring onions, or thinnings are delicious in salads. Sliced onion can be boiled or tossed gently in hot fat until limp and transparent, or fried a crisp brown.

Onions with Mushroom Stuffing: Large onions can be peeled and parboiled, then the centres removed and replaced with a stuffing made of fresh white breadcrumbs mixed with an equal quantity of chopped mushrooms. Dot with butter and bake for about 1 hour, in a moderate oven, basting occasionally.

Pickled Onions with Beef: Cut 2 lb. good quality stewing steak in large dice, and seal all over in hot butter in a flameproof pan. When the meat changes colour, add 4 large pickled onions, chopped, and 1 tablespoon vinegar from the jar. Pour in ¼ pint water and cover. Simmer until beef is tender. Taste and add salt and pepper to season. Serve each person with a good mound of mashed potato, hollowed out in the middle and filled with the beef.

143

Orange and Onion Salad: Wash and dry thoroughly a lettuce, some endive or chicory. Tear into small pieces and place in a salad bowl. Peel 3 oranges and cut into crosswise slices. Arrange over the salad greens and top with wafer-thin rings from a small-sized onion. Combine well together 3 tablespoons lemon juice, 4 tablespoons salad oil, ½ teaspoon garlic salt, ½ teaspoon salt, ½ teaspoon powder mustard and 1 teaspoon sugar. Pour over salad, and toss lightly before serving.

Parsnips: These were well known and popular in England before the potato arrived. They were used as a base for a sweet pudding flavoured with honey and spice, as well as a savoury vegetable. As vegetables they are best left till after the first hard frost, when the roots become mellow and golden. They are good browned in the roasting tin with the joint. Cut into 'chips' and boiled for a few minutes, then well dried and tossed in flour, they can be fried in deep fat until crisp golden.

Parsnip Cakes: Combine 1 lb. cooked, mashed parsnips with 1½ teaspoons salt, ¼ teaspoon black pepper, 1 teaspoon sugar, 1 teaspoon paprika, 1 teaspoon lemon juice, 1 egg, 2 oz. breadcrumbs. Mix well and shape into 2½-inch rounds about ½ inch thick. Dip in flour and fry in very hot fat till brown. Serve hot.

Glazed Parsnips: Quarter 8 boiled parsnips and place them in a fireproof dish. Dot with butter or margarine. Mix 2 tablespoons soft brown sugar with ½ teaspoon powdered mustard and sprinkle over the top. Bake in a preheated moderately hot oven for 20 minutes or until parsnips are glazed and browned.

Peas: Young, they should be cooked a few minutes in quickly boiling water with a sprig of mint and a teaspoon sugar. Drain and eat immediately. Older peas require to be cooked more slowly with a little sugar and salt added to the water. Serve tossed in melted butter with mint. Almost a sacrilege, but a tiny pinch of bicarbonate of soda added to the water does tenderise peas.

French-style Peas: Shell 1½ lb. young peas. Wash the heart of a lettuce and put it into a saucepan, add the peas, 3 teaspoons chopped spring onions, 4 teaspoons chopped mint, a pinch of salt and one of sugar, and dot with pieces of butter. Put on lid of saucepan and place over low heat. Shake pan frequently at first; after a few minutes peas will be cooking in moisture from the lettuce and melted butter. They should cook in 5–7 minutes. Serve with the onion and lettuce.

Pea-Pod Soup: The pods, which are usually thrown away, contain a lot of goodness and flavour, and should always be utilised to make a vegetable stock for gravies, or a soup. Throw away any that are damaged or withered, and wash the remainder well. Put in a large pan, cover with water, put on the lid and simmer for about an hour. Strain off all the liquid, pressing the pods down well in a strainer to extract the juice. The addition of a stock cube will quickly turn the liquid into a clear pea soup.

Purée of Peas: Make about ½ lb. floury cooked potato, and put it through a sieve. Cook 2 lb. shelled young peas in the usual way, drain and return to the pan with 2 oz. butter, 1 tablespoon very finely chopped onion and a little salt and pepper. Add as much strong chicken stock as the peas will absorb, about 4 tablespoons. Sieve or liquidise, and beat gradually into the potato until it forms a solid purée. Serve as for pease pudding.

Potatoes: New potatoes, freshly lifted, should only require the skins to be rubbed off under running water, and boiling for about 12 minutes in salted water with a sprig of mint. Older ones need scraping, or the skins removed after boiling, but do not peel them. It is a pity to peel potatoes as larger ones are better baked.

Punch-nep: This is made by beating together equal quantities of mashed potatoes and turnips which have been boiled separately. Add butter to taste and plenty of seasoning.

Potato Cake: Here is a use for potatoes too small to bake which really need peeling. Peel and slice 4 medium size potatoes. Melt 1 oz. butter and 1 tablespoon oil in a thick frying pan, pack the slices in thin layers, seasoning with salt and pepper. Cover with a plate, fry over low heat for 15 minutes. Turn over on plate, slip back into pan for a further 10 minutes or until tender.

Broxty: Grate raw potato into enough hot milk to cover. Cook till hot, soft and firm. Season. Pile into a mound on a hot dish; make a deep well in the centre and pour in very hot bacon fat or melted butter. Eat with a fork, Stirring the potato into the fat.

Potato and Onion Pancakes: Mix well 12 oz. fluffy, mashed potatoes, 1 tablespoon minced onion, 1 teaspoon salt, ¼ teaspoon ground black pepper, ½ teaspoon finely chopped thyme, ½ garlic clove, crushed, 1 oz. sieved plain flour with a beaten egg. Blend in a good ¼ pint milk. Drop tablespoons of this batter on to a lightly buttered girdle. Cook over medium heat, turning to brown both sides. Can be served with bacon and apple sauce.

Potato Soup

1 LB. POTATOES	SALT AND PEPPER
1 ONION	SINGLE CREAM
1 PINT STOCK OR WATER	FRIED CROÛTONS
3 TEASPOONS FLOUR BLENDED	CHERVIL
WITH MILK	

Wash potatoes, peel onion and slice. Simmer in the stock until the vegetables are soft. Rub through a sieve and return to the stove with the blended flour and salt and pepper to taste. Bring to the boil and serve in hot soup plates. Add a little cream, fried croûtons and 1 teaspoon chopped chervil to each serving.

Radishes: To make radish roses, trim and cut in various shapes as shown below, put in iced water to open out.

Salsify: This used to be more widely used than it is now, and has been called the vegetable oyster. Its flowers are pretty enough for the flower border. The root should be lifted and scraped with care. It is boiled or steamed and afterwards fried an appetising brown. Or it can be served in its cooking liquor thickened into a creamy sauce, accentuating the vegetable's unusual and interesting flavour. Sometimes it is egg-and-breadcrumbed before frying, and served with slices of lemon, like fillets of fish.

Spinach: Needs to be washed well to remove all grit, and as it cooks down allow about 8 oz. per person. Pick off the coarse stalks and pack into a saucepan with only the water that clings to the leaves. Heat gently, turning leaves over occasionally, then bring to the boil and cook gently until soft, 10–15 minutes. Drain thoroughly and re-heat with a knob of butter, salt and pepper.

Creamed Spinach: Sieve the cooked spinach, add 1–2 tablespoons cream, salt and pepper and re-heat before serving.

Spinach Cheese Puffs

6 OZ. COOKED AND WELL-DRAINED SPINACH	$\frac{1}{8}$ TEASPOON GROUND BLACK -PEPPER
2 EGGS, BEATEN	3 OZ. GRATED CHEDDAR CHEESE
4 OZ. FINE BREADCRUMBS	
2 TABLESPOONS LEMON JUICE	1 EGG, BEATEN
2 TEASPOONS MINCED ONION	1 TABLESPOON MILK
1 TEASPOON SALT	1 OZ. FINE BREADCRUMBS
$\frac{1}{4}$ TEASPOON NUTMEG	

Sieve or chop spinach very finely. Blend in with the 2 eggs, 4 oz. breadcrumbs, lemon juice, onion, salt, nutmeg, pepper and cheese. Shape into 1½-inch rounds. Mix remaining egg with the milk and dip the puffs in this. Then roll them in breadcrumbs. Fry in hot, deep fat until brown and crisp. Drain on crumpled kitchen paper. Serve hot.

Tomatoes: To skin them easily, scald them in boiling water for 1 minute. Slice with the core to keep in the juice for sandwiches, and remove the core to loosen the juice for chopping and cooking.

Tomato Salad: Wash 6 firm, ripe tomatoes, cut into 1-inch cubes and toss lightly into a dressing made with $\frac{1}{8}$ teaspoon garlic salt, $\frac{1}{2}$ teaspoon salt, $\frac{1}{2}$ teaspoon sugar, $\frac{1}{2}$ teaspoon ground black pepper, $\frac{1}{2}$ teaspoon chopped oregano (or marjoram), $\frac{1}{2}$ teaspoon chopped basil, 1 teaspoon cider vinegar, 2 tablespoons olive or salad oil. Chill 30 minutes. Serve sprinkled with nasturtium seeds or capers as a salad with lettuce.

Baked Stuffed Tomatoes: Prepare as above. Use the pulp up for sauces or soups. Fill the centre with a savoury egg custard, add a pinch of dried or a teaspoon of fresh herbs to the filling of each tomato. Put on a greased baking tray in a moderate oven for 30 minutes or until the custard is set. Cooked rice mixed with grated cheese and a little beaten egg makes another good filling. Small amounts of left-over cold meat can be converted into a main meal if minced, mixed with enough gravy to moisten, and used to stuff tomatoes. Add Worcestershire sauce or tomato ketchup if liked.

Tomatoes in Batter: Some people find Toad-in-the-Hole too rich and prefer this version. Make up a Yorkshire pudding mixture, with a little more flour than usual. Put 6 pork sausages and 6 large tomatoes in a roasting tin with 1 oz. lard, put in a hot oven for 5 minutes, then pour the batter round them. Bake until well risen and brown, serve each person 1 sausage and 1 tomato with batter.

Turnips: Small white turnips should be boiled whole in salted water until just tender and served with plenty of butter and some pepper or nutmeg. Larger turnips should be boiled and mashed like swedes, and served together with them, in alternate golden and orange heaps, as the flavours go so well together. Make the top glisten with melted bacon fat or good dripping.

Turnips with Bacon and Dill: Place 3 lb. peeled, diced turnips with 2 teaspoons sugar, $1\frac{1}{2}$ teaspoons salt, $\frac{1}{2}$ teaspoon dill seed in a saucepan with 1 inch boiling water. Cover, bring to boil, and cook 10 minutes. Drain. Mix vegetables with 5 tablespoons sour cream, $\frac{1}{8}$ teaspoon ground black pepper, 2 teaspoons lemon juice. Bake in a covered casserole until turnips are tender (about 20 minutes in a moderate oven). Cook 6 rashers of bacon until half done. Arrange on casserole and grill to crisp.

Household Uses

Cooking vegetables: Use as little water as possible to avoid washing away valuable mineral salts and vitamins, as well as losing much of the flavour. Farmers' wives have always set a good example by using vegetable water to make sauces, gravies and soups.

Carrot Juice: Carrots have a high natural sugar content and in times of scarcity have been used to replace fruit in sweet dishes. They are recommended to improve sight, and as recently as World War Two, to cure night blindness.

Celery Broth: Celery is particularly rich in vitamins and minerals. A celery broth is a better nightcap for people with rheumatic tendencies, or for those who wish to lose weight, than a milky drink. Celeriac has the same properties.

Vegetable Juices: Freshly extracted they have a high nutritive value, but many of them are unpalatable alone. The juices of such vegetables as cabbage, spinach or beetroot can always be combined with carrot or tomato juice to make a refreshing health drink.

An Old Sleeping Potion: Juice of lettuce is one of the oldest soporifics. Lettuce was pounded with pestle and mortar to extract the milky juice, which was dried, made into cakes and given as a mild anaesthetic. Country housewives used to lay a lettuce leaf over a fractious baby's mouth to soothe it to sleep.

Nettles: Improve the quality of the blood because they contain iron. They can be used as a flavouring in salt-reduced and diabetic diets, as nettles contain a salt which is not water-retaining.

Onions stewed in milk and butter and eaten hot were a farmhouse remedy for a cold on the chest.

Skins of onions should not be thrown away. They are a good natural colouring for soups and stews. Broth can be improved in colour by cooking the skins in it.

Coloured Easter Eggs: Cut onion skins into interesting patterns, wrap them round eggs with a wet cloth and hard-boil the eggs. Allow to get cold in cold water then polish with a little butter or oil, and you will have an attractive mottled, striped or marbled gold-and-brown egg. For a clear yellow-coloured egg, boil the skins loose in the water with the eggs.

To avoid tears when peeling onions, cover them in water and peel them under water.

For Rheumatism: A potato carried on the person is supposed to be a cure for rheumatism. A small potato should be carried in the pocket during the day and at night tied loosely to a wrist in a stocking; discard it for another when it becomes shrivelled.

Seed Potatoes: Planted in ground which has been untended and weed-ridden will help clear the ground of weeds.

Colds in the Head and Neuralgia: They are said to be cured by scraping horse-radish which causes copious tears.

Horse-radish Embrocation: The expressed juice made into an emulsion with the yolk of an egg is a country embrocation for rheumatism.

Appendix

Freezing garden produce

Home freezer owners find it especially worthwhile to grow their own fruit and vegetables, because the occasional glut is no longer a problem. Preserving by canning or bottling is a lengthy business, and in the case of some vegetables not always satisfactory or even safe. It is so easy to freeze down surplus produce, and with care the results are equal to the expensive commercially frozen packs. For a small outlay you can enjoy fruits and vegetables of your own growing all the year round. However, since frozen food is kept far longer and therefore at a much lower temperature than in the domestic refrigerator, it requires special protection against dehydration by the cold, dry air inside the freezer.

Foods with a relatively high water content are liable to suffer damage to the cell structure, during the freezing process. Water, which expands on freezing, ruptures the cell walls as it passes through the temperature zone round 32°F. Quick freezing minimises the extent of the damage.

Fruit and vegetables, being foods with a relatively high water content, need careful preparation and packing.

How freezing preserves food

Freezing is the most natural of all forms of food preservation. It works quite simply, by reducing the temperature of food below the level at which bacteria are active; they become dormant, thus preventing any further deterioration. Not destroyed, merely *dormant*; which means the food must be extremely clean and fresh, and handled under the most hygienic conditions when prepared for freezing. Then the thawing process, which again raises the temperature to the zone of bacterial activity, will not wake a host of slumbering bacteria at the same time!

General rules for freezing

1. Choose only fruit and vegetables for freezing which are in peak condition. Set aside any which are either slightly under or over ripe for immediate eating, and do not be tempted to eat the perfect specimens and freeze down the rest.

2. Prepare for freezing as soon as possible after picking. This prevents unnecessary loss of vitamin C, from vegetables especially, and arrests deterioration at the earliest possible stage.

3. Wash fruit only if absolutely necessary and in the case of berry fruits hull after washing, to keep interior of fruit as dry as possible. Keep your hands, any implements used, and the packing materials perfectly clean to prevent bacterial contamination in the interim period between picking and freezing down.

4. Pack food in moisture-vapour-proof materials, capable of preventing the invasion of dry air into the pack or loss of moisture from the pack itself into the cabinet. Those I prefer include polythene containers with snap-on seals, guaranteed not to split or warp at sub-zero temperatures, such as Tupperware, heavy-gauge foil and shaped foil containers.

5. Wrap or pack to eliminate airspaces, other than the necessary headspace to allow for the expansion of the water content of the food on freezing. Unnecessary airspaces allow moisture to be drawn out of the food and cause frost formation inside the pack.

6. Containers with seals and sheet aluminium foil do not require sealing. If needed, use freezer tape for parcels (ordinary sealing tapes crack at low temperature), twist ties for bags. Label with self-adhesive labels, as gummed labels peel off, and using chinagraph or crayon pencil state contents and date frozen. If packs are liable to be removed by inexperienced cooks, give brief details of defrosting time and cooking method required. Some housewives find it useful to identify those packs, which other members of the family may remove, with a coloured label.

7. Freeze down fast, immediately after packing. Cool vegetables for packing, as quickly as possible after blanching. Put the packs into the fast-freezing compartment, throw the fast-freeze switch or merely lower the temperature dial, according to your type of freezer. Restore to normal (between 0°F and −5°F) when frozen, 2–20 hours according to type and number of packs.

8. Keep packs fully frozen until required. Avoid partially defrosting and then re-freezing.

Packing fruit for the freezer

Most fruits, other than very watery ones such as melon, freeze well. Fruit quickly loses vitamin C after packing, and some fruit tends to discolour when the flesh is exposed to the air. The addition of $\frac{1}{4}$ teaspoon ascorbic acid to half a pint of cold water replaces lost vitamin C and prevents discolouration, but the following methods are more popular from the point of view of preserving the natural flavour.

1. Open freezing.
2. Dry sugar pack.
3. Sugar syrup pack.
4. Cooked fruit purée pack.

One pound of fresh fruit, with its own juice or in a sugar syrup, makes an average serving for four.

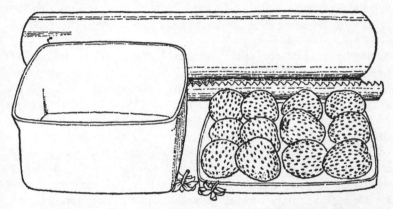

Open freezing: Use this method for soft juicy fruits especially delicate berries which damage easily, such as strawberries, raspberries, blackberries and loganberries. Ensure that, by spreading the fruit out on trays, each berry freezes separately, and therefore more quickly than if packed together. (Tight packing during freezing down causes squashing and damage of the lower layers of fruit.) Spread dry, clean berries on trays or Tupperware seals, freeze at lowest temperature possible until hard, about 1 hour for small berries, 2 hours for strawberries. Pack at once into polythene containers with a rigid base to distribute the weight of the fruit, and foil dividers between the layers; or in heavy-gauge polythene bags, also with dividers. Seal bags with twist ties. Label, return to freezer.

Note: The frozen fruit will not at first appear any different, but do not wait until a bloom caused by condensation appears on the surface, as it would do after a few minutes.

Dry Sugar Pack: Use this method for most fruits. It is particularly suitable for soft juicy berries; currants and gooseberries. Also good for sliced apples, apricots, plums and greengages, although apples tend to discolour. Allow 1 lb. sugar for 3–5 lb. fruit, according to its natural sweetness. Spoon alternate layers of fruit and sugar into containers, or place all the clean fruit with the sugar in a bowl. Turn the fruit gently with a wooden spoon until all is lightly coated, then pack, leave a ½-inch headspace, snap on seal, or seal polythene bags with twist ties. Label and freeze. Foil or waxed cartons may be used but should be sealed with freezer tape. A date on the label is particularly important so that early varieties which were frozen first can be used up first. Foil dividers to prevent crushing by weight are also desirable with this method.

Sugar Syrup Pack: Use this method for less delicate fruits. It is particularly suitable for: stoned fruit such as plums, greengages, apricots and cherries; also for rhubarb, citrus fruit, apples, pears, currants, pineapples and peaches. Prepare the fruit; if washing it drain well. Remove stones from plums, etc.; peel citrus fruits and divide into segments; blanch cut rhubarb, also peeled, cored and sliced apples, in boiling water for 1 minute; peel pineapple, remove core and eyes, and peel and stone peaches. Fruits which discolour quickly, such as apples, peaches and apricots, should be dipped in lemon juice or put into salt water or ascorbic acid solution (¼ teaspoon crystals in 4 tablespoons water). Pack into polythene containers, bags or wax cartons. Pour over cold sugar syrup, allowing ¼ pint syrup to each 1 pint pack of fruit. Make syrup well beforehand and chill in refrigerator. For a medium syrup suitable for most fruits, dissolve 11 oz. sugar in 1 pint hot water. For a thin syrup suitable for delicately flavoured fruit, use sugar in proportion of 7 oz. to 1 pint water. Syrup should just cover fruit. Allow ½-inch headspace and, if necessary to hold fruit under syrup, place a layer of crumpled foil on top. Seal and label.

Cooked Fruit Purée Pack: Use this method for fresh soft berry fruits or other fruit that can be stewed and made into purée. Fresh berries can be puréed, uncooked, with sugar. Cook other fruits with sugar, and then purée. This can be done either with a sieve or electric blender. Some fruit purées such as apple, which may be required for unsweetened dishes, can be labelled and frozen separately. Stoned fruits should be sliced and cooked, with 4 tablespoons water to each 1 lb. prepared fruit, to a pulp over gentle heat. Cool cooked pulps quickly. Pack prepared purée into suitable containers leaving ½-inch headspace. Seal and label. It is particularly useful, when freezing purées, to pack some in small containers, so that you always have a supply of baby food in suitable quantities. Or you may want in the case of apple purée, to use it as apple sauce.

Packing vegetables for the freezer

All those vegetables which are usually served cooked freeze well. Large, woody root vegetables are the least satisfactory. Do not freeze salad vegetables, or others with a high water content. Vegetables, unlike fruit, are a non-acidic food, and require the extra precaution of blanching before freezing to halt destructive enzyme action. The blanching process is extremely easy to carry out, preserves the bright colour, softens vegetables and makes them easier to pack, and also shortens cooking time when thawed.

Blanching Vegetables: Prepare the vegetables as for cooking. You will need a large saucepan (the gallon size blanches 1 lb. vegetables at a time). Put vegetables into a wire basket and lower into fast-boiling water, or put straight into water. Allow water to return to the boil, then time blanching from that moment according to the following chart. Accuracy of timing is important.

155

Insufficient blanching time may not halt enzyme activity, and over-blanching may spoil the texture and flavour of vegetables. Remove wire basket from saucepan, place under running cold water from the tap, then plunge into a bowl of cold water, chilled if possible by the addition of ice cubes. Alternatively, transfer vegetables straight from the saucepan with a perforated draining spoon to a colander and cool as above.

BLANCHING TIMETABLE

Vegetable	Minutes	Vegetable	Minutes
Asparagus, small		Brussels sprouts,	
spears	2	medium	4
Asparagus, large		Cabbage, sliced	1½
spears	3	Carrots, diced	3
Artichokes	5–7	Carrots, whole	5
Aubergines	4	Cauliflower, florets	3
Beans, broad	3	Celery, sliced	3
Beans, French or		Corn on the cob	5–8
runner, whole	2–3	Courgettes, sliced	2
Beans, French or		Parsnips, diced	2
runner, sliced	1	Peas	1–1½
Broccoli	3–4	Spinach	2

When vegetables are completely cold, drain thoroughly and pack as for fruit. That is, putting delicate vegetables like peas, whenever possible, in rigid-bottomed containers to distribute the weight, with ½-inch headspace and with foil dividers half way up the packs. If using polythene bags, do not fill more than two-thirds full; to close, bring together and gently press out as much air as possible without damaging the contents. Seal with twist ties. Putting the date on the label is important to ensure that early processed packs are used up first.

Methods of packing

As for fruit, there are various methods of packing vegetables after the essential blanching process.
1. Open freezing.
2. Dry pack.
3. Brine pack.

Open Freezing: Delicate vegetables can be open frozen in the same way as delicate fruits, but may require scraping off the freezing trays. The advantage is that small amounts of vegetables may be removed from the pack while still in the frozen state.

Dry Pack: Simply pack well-drained vegetables into containers as soon as they are cold.

Brine Pack: Some vegetables, especially green beans, tend to toughen when frozen. As brine tends to soften them it should only be used for these and other less delicate vegetables, and do not add salt when cooking. Make up a brine by dissolving 2 tablespoons salt in 1 quart of hot water, cool and use chilled.

Note: Vegetables require $\frac{1}{4}$–$\frac{1}{2}$ inch headspace according to the closeness of packing. Carrots sliced in rings pack closely together, and so require a little headspace. Cauliflower florets cannot be so closely packed, therefore no headspace is needed.

Defrosting frozen fruit and vegetables

The storage life of most fruits, other than citrus fruits, packed in sugar or syrup is 9–12 months. Fruit packed dry without sugar or in the form of purée will keep for 6–8 months. Most vegetables, however packed, have a storage life of 10–12 months. Spinach, if frozen as a purée, will only keep 6–8 months. Vegetables are usually cooked from the frozen state and therefore require no defrosting, apart from corn on the cob which should be thawed first.

Preparing fruit for use: All fruit other than purées should be allowed to thaw for about 3 hours (according to the size of pack) at room temperature, or 6 hours in the refrigerator. The texture is best if eaten while slightly frozen or well-chilled. To hasten thawing, airtight packs such as sealed polythene containers can be placed under running cold water for about $\frac{1}{2}$ an hour, then turned out and carefully broken up with a fork to thaw the centre of the pack. Purées, to be used in cooked dishes, can be thawed quickly by placing the airtight pack in a bowl of warm water.

Preparing vegetables for use: Cook from the frozen state or partly thawed. Blanched vegetables which were, ideally, young and tender when picked require very little further cooking. Cook with the minimum amount of water, covered, for half the usual cooking time or less. Delicate vegetables such as peas only require to be placed over moderate heat in a covered pan with salt, pepper and a knob of butter for about 5 minutes.

Recommended varieties to grow for freezing

Strawberries: Cambridge Vigour, Cambridge Rival, Cambridge Favourite, Talisman, Royal Sovereign, Cambridge Late Pine.

Blackcurrants: Laxton's Giant, Malvern Cross and Blacksmith.

Currants: Red Lake, White Leviathan.

Raspberries: Norfolk Giant, Lloyd George, Malling Enterprise, Malling Jewel, Malling Promise.

Plums and Gages: Victoria, Cambridge Gage, Comte d'Althan's Gage, Jefferson.

Apples: Bramley Seedling.

Stringless and Runner Beans: Tendergreen, Tenderlong, Emerge, Emperor, Crusader and Ne Plus Ultra.

Carrots: Early Nantes, Gem and James Scarlet Intermediate.

Corn on the Cob: John Innes Hybrid.

Peas: Early Onward, Foremost.

Spinach: Goliath, New Zealand.

Brussels Sprouts: Cambridge No. 3, Cambridge Special, Irish Elegance, Jade Cross, Victory Freezer Pea.

Freezing Herbs: Fresh herbs, e.g. parsley, chives, fennel, mint, basil, thyme, can be frozen for use in cooking. Pick just before flowering, strip off any woody stalks, wash and shake dry the leaves or leafy sprigs. Seal in small polythene bags or containers, or lay flat on one half of a sheet of foil, and press the other half over to form a flat pack, crimping the edges tightly. When required, thaw whole leaves, or crumble frozen leaves to save chopping.

BIBLIOGRAPHY

VEGETABLE GARDEN DISPLAYED, Royal Horticultural Society (Bles), 60p
GARDEN DESIGN, W. Midgley (Penguin) 62½p
AMATEUR GARDENING POCKET GUIDE, A. G. L. Hellyer (Collingridge) 95p
RARE VEGETABLES FOR GARDEN AND TABLE, J. Organ (Faber), £1·50

Recipe Index